ART ON WINGS

Celebrating the Reunification of a Triptych by Gerard David

Ariane van Suchtelen

Yvette Bruijnen

Edwin Buijsen

MAURITSHUIS, THE HAGUE

V+K PUBLISHING/INMERC, BUSSUM

© 1997 V+K Publishing, Bussum
Mauritshuis, The Hague

ISBN 90 66 11 831 8
NUGI 921

This catalogue has been published to coincide with the exhibition of the
same title, Mauritshuis, The Hague
1 March - 22 June 1997

ILLUSTRATIONS
Gerard David, *Triptych with the Nativity, Donors and Saints* and *Forest
Scene* (cat. 1)
(front cover (detail centre piece), back cover (outside wings), front flap
(left wing), back flap (right wing))
p. 39: Master of the Solomon Triptych, *Triptych with the Story of Solomon*
(cat. 7, detail of right wing)

Contents

4 FOREWORD
   Frederik J. Duparc

6 INTRODUCTION
   Ariane van Suchtelen

11 CELEBRATING THE REUNIFICATION OF
    GERARD DAVID'S TRIPTYCH
    Yvette Bruijnen

24 CONSIDERING THE OX AND THE ASS
    IN SEARCH OF AN INTERPRETATION
    FOR GERARD DAVID'S *FOREST SCENE*
    Edwin Buijsen

39 CATALOGUE
    Ariane van Suchtelen

    1 Gerard David
    2 Hans Memling
    3 Jan Provoost
    4 Unknown master from Brussels
    5 Master of Frankfurt
    6 Unknown master from Antwerp or Zeeland
    7 Master of the Solomon Triptych
    8 Unknown painter and sculptor from Haarlem
    9 Master of Alkmaar
    10 Hans Suess von Kulmbach

90 BIBLIOGRAPHY

FOREWORD

The Mauritshuis in The Hague owes its fame chiefly to its collection of Dutch and Flemish paintings from the seventeenth century. However, the collection boasts far more than this, including important fifteenth- and sixteenth-century Flemish and German paintings. The *Lamentation of Christ* by Rogier van der Weyden, as well as the portraits by Hans Holbein the Younger, clearly belong to the highlights of early painted art in Dutch public collections. The portraits were already part of the stadholder's collection, forming the basis of the present collection in the Mauritshuis, while the painting by Van der Weyden was acquired for the museum in 1827 during the reign of Willem I.

One of the aims of the exhibition policy of the Mauritshuis is to draw attention to the range and variety of its permanent collection. The exhibition *Art on Wings* will show some of the oldest paintings in the Mauritshuis as well as some loans, in such a way as to illustrate their original religious function and setting in a more effective manner than is normally found in museums nowadays. Although objects in a museum can rarely be displayed in their original context, in the case of diptychs and triptychs – or parts of these – that are the theme of this exhibition, this sense of alienation has serious consequences. It is common in museums to hang panels that are painted on both sides flat against the wall, so that only one side is on view. In order to offer visitors a better idea of what the object originally looked like, the present exhibition will display most of the pieces in a three-dimensional fashion.

An exhibition and the publication that attends it always result from the work of many people. The present show was the idea of Edwin Buijsen, who until January 1995 was curator of exhibitions at the Mauritshuis, and is presently curator at the Netherlands Institute for Art History in The Hague (RKD). His plan was taken up and elaborated by the present curator of exhibitions, Ariane van Suchtelen, who assumed the lion's share in preparing both the exhibition and related publication. We are delighted that both Edwin Buijsen and Yvette Bruijnen were able to write an article on the central work in this show, the reunified triptych by Gerard David (cat. 1). Yvette Bruijnen discusses the materials and painterly aspects, while Edwin Buijsen expands on the meaning of the representation and the original function of the altarpiece.

4

Conservators from the restoration department carried out research into technical aspects of several paintings. A number of paintings included in the exhibition were restored, namely cat. 3 by Carol Pottasch and Jørgen Wadum, cat. 6 by Geraldine van Heemstra, cat. 7 by Petria Noble and cat. 10 by Mireille te Marvelde. In addition, many of the staff of the Mauritshuis Museum have given invaluable assistance with this project.

The starting point for the exhibition was the collection in the Mauritshuis, which includes several long-term loans from the Rijksmuseum. A small number of other loans enriched the scene. We are most grateful to The Metropolitan Museum of Art in New York for their loan which made the reconstruction of the David triptych possible. We should also like to express warm thanks to the National Gallery of Ireland, Dublin, to the Rijksmuseum in Amsterdam, and to a private lender, who wishes to remain anonymous.

Many people assisted in this project. We should like to mention in particular: Maryan Ainsworth, Professor J.R.J. van Asperen de Boer, George Bisacca, Martin Bijl, Peter van den Brink, Andrew O'Connor, David Crombie, Liesbeth Eijl, Rudi Ekkart, Everett Fahy, Jan Piet Filedt Kok, Raymond Keaveney, Wouter Kloek, Lambert Muller, Jacqueline Ridge, Catherine Stainer-Hutchins, J.J. Susijn and Manja Zeldenrust.

The collaboration with V+K Publishing has once more produced a catalogue that is both attractively presented and contains a wealth of interesting detail.

The Mauritshuis is always dependent upon external financing, also for small exhibitions. We are delighted to report that our own Foundation, the Friends of the Mauritshuis, has supported the exhibition with a more than generous contribution.

Frederik J. Duparc
Director

INTRODUCTION

Ariane van Suchtelen

It is a sobering thought that so little remains today of all the wealth of art production from the past. This certainly holds for the more distant past, the works of the late Middle Ages which are the theme of the exhibition *Art on Wings*. In many cases only parts of these works have survived the ravages of time (cat. 2, 4, 6, 9 and 10). It was quite common for the panels of a diptych or triptych to be acquired by different collectors (cat. 1, 4, 5 and 10).

Only in exceptional cases has the loss of an important work of art been recorded. Thus we find Karel van Mander (1548-1606) writing in his *Schilder-boeck* of 1604 that the famous Haarlem artist Geertgen tot Sint Jans (1460/65-c.1495) had painted an altarpiece for the Order of St John in his native town. It was 'a large and magnificent piece, presenting the Crucifixion. The wings were also large, and painted on both sides. One wing and the central panel were destroyed in the Iconoclastic Fury [1566] or in the city siege [Siege of Haarlem, 1572-73]. The wing that was left over was sawn through the middle and now there are two beautiful pieces'.[1] It is undoubtedly a stroke of good fortune that the right-hand wing from this once so impressive triptych – almost six metres wide when it was open – has been preserved. The front and

back of this wing now form two separate paintings in the Vienna Kunsthistorisches Museum (figs 1 and 2).[2] A similar fate was suffered by many late-medieval paintings, though it was not always war, discord or conflagration that destroyed works of art. It was not uncommon for diptychs and triptychs to be taken apart when they no longer served their original purpose, so that the panels could be sold separately. Indeed, in the nineteenth and twentieth century it became common practice to saw apart the front and reverse sides of painted panels of altarpieces. In this way two works of art could be made out of one panel and put on the market as separate paintings.

The late medieval paintings that found their way into museums and private collections are prized in the first place for their artistic merit. Their religious function has long been lost, although that was the original reason both for their creation and for their form and content. These works of art were originally intended to be used either as altarpieces – in churches or cloisters, or for private devotion. But since museums are not churches this religious purpose has gradually become disregarded.

Traditional art-historical research describes the history of artists and their œuvres and analyses

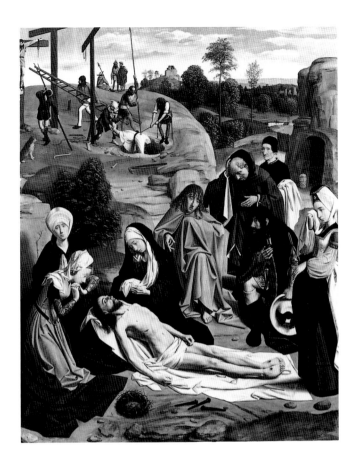

1 Geertgen tot Sint Jans,
The Lamentation. *Panel,*
172 × 139 cm. Kunsthistorisches
Museum, Vienna.

2 Geertgen tot Sint Jans,
The Roman Emperor Julian the
Apostate orders the Burning of
John the Baptist's Bones. *Panel,*
172 × 139 cm. Kunsthistorisches
Museum, Vienna.

3 *Rogier van der Weyden,* Triptych with the Seven Sacraments *(detail from the centre panel). Museum voor Schone Kunsten, Antwerp.*

4 *Anonymous Master, Reliquary Chest, c.1275. Abbey Church, Doberan.*

representations (the iconography). However, over the past few decades the study of the original function of works of art has become increasingly important. Several key questions arise in this discussion. First, where was the work originally intended to be placed (for example, in a church) and what was the significance and function of the work in this setting? Then, who were the patrons or donors and what was their motivation? In this context we can understand the importance nowadays attached to having the original frame for a painting. In the rare cases when these have been preserved they are quite correctly considered to be an important and inextricable part of the work of art (cat. 3 and 7).

The exhibition *Art on Wings*, which is concerned with the original context of a piece, fits into the current trend that seeks to reunite (temporarily) sections of works

of art that have become separated and dispersed. A fine example of an exhibition that reunited several 'lost limbs' was the one held in the Rijksmuseum, Amsterdam in 1994-95, titled *The Art of Devotion*. Central in this exhibition was the function of works of art in private devotion. In *Art on Wings* the emphasis lies on altarpieces, that is, works intended more for public display (cat. 1, 4, 5, 6, 9 and 10).[3]

In early Christian times the altar table was only used during the religious service as a place on which to lay liturgical items such as holy books or the chalice. During the service the priest stood behind the altar table, so that no large objects could be placed on the altar – otherwise he would not remain in full view of the believers. During the eleventh century it became customary for the priest

8

to stand in the space between the congregation and the altar which made it possible to place decorative objects on the altar. The altar decorations could thus form an appropriate background for the celebration of the Mass: a fitting visual setting for the holy moment of transubstantiation, when the bread and wine change for the believer into the body and blood of Christ (fig. 3). In this moment Christ's sacrifice of his life upon the Cross to redeem mankind from the stain of original sin is continually repeated and remembered.

Only gradually did the altarpiece gain an accepted place upon the altar. The development of this during the Middle Ages is an intricate story. It is connected not only with the position of the priest, either behind or in front of the altar during the Mass, but also with the changing role of relics and reliquaries that were placed upon the altar. In AD 787 at the Council of Nicaea it was determined that every altar should be dedicated to a particular saint and should contain a holy relic. It gradually became the custom to place relics on the altar during the Mass and on solemn occasions. With the growth of relic worship, the reliquaries became more important and they often acquired elaborate forms. In Germany, for instance, in the course of the thirteenth century large retables presenting religious scenes were made to hold relics. The Synod of Trier held in 1310 gave considerable stimulation to the presentation of pictorial scenes on altars by decreeing that an inscription, a statue or a picture should make it apparent which saint the altar was dedicated to. In the course of the thirteenth and fourteenth century the pictorial representations gradually became more important as visual attractions on the altar, and the relics themselves diminished in significance.

During the fifteenth century the number of altars in churches rose appreciably, thereby increasing the demand for altarpieces. At the beginning of the fifteenth century there were 37 altars in the cathedral of Sint Jan in 's-Hertogenbosch, while about one hundred years later there were 52.[4] A growing number of professional and religious societies such as guilds and brotherhoods founded their own altars (cat. 6). When it was the feast of their patron saint or when a member of the society died, Mass would be celebrated at the altar. Also, the number of private family chapels in churches increased, each one having its own altar (cat. 1 and 9).

In the late Middle Ages the most usual type of altarpiece in the Netherlands was a triptych with a painted centre panel and side panels painted on front and reverse, which covered the centre panel when closed. The earliest known (southern Netherlandish) examples of this type date from about 1390.[5] This kind of altarpiece, or retable, probably developed primarily from reliquary chests with painted doors. A small number of thirteenth-century German reliquaries of this kind have been preserved, such as the chest from the church of the Cistercian abbey of Doberan, near Schwerin (fig. 4).[6] This piece, dating from about 1275, contains several compartments to hold relics. The chest has painted wooden doors that served to protect the precious contents. The figures of John the Baptist and St John the Evangelist decorate the inside of these doors.

The wings of triptychs also served to protect the inside. Therefore it is frequently found that the painting on the outside of the wings is more damaged than that on the inside and on the centre panel. Moreover, the wings play an important role in the narrative sequence of the triptych, of which the various scenes cannot be assimilated at one glance. The hierarchical nature of the different scenes is often expressed through the monochrome painting on the outside of the wings, contrasting with the wealth of colour on the inside (cat. 6). Indeed, the outside wings often serve as introduction to the central scene which is revealed when the leaves are opened. For instance, the outside wings will often present the Annunciation. The announcement of the coming of the Saviour is a highly appropriate preparation for the scenes from the life of Christ that will appear on the inside. Furthermore, the outside of the wings would often be used to present pictures of saints or the coats of arms of the donors (cat. 9). Almost nothing is known with certainty of the original practices concerning opening and shutting these altarpieces. Clearly, however, the presence of wings offers dramatic possibilities of concealing and revealing the main scene.

Although the altarpiece has no role as such in the liturgy of the Mass, the subject matter of the presentation is obviously closely connected with its function as adornment on the altar. Sometimes the saint to whom the altar was dedicated played the key role in the presentation. However, generally speaking all scenes connected with Christ's life and Passion form a fitting background to the celebration of Eucharist.

When altarpieces and works of art intended for private devotion were placed in museum collections, they lost all their religious functions. The panels by Gerard David with a wooded landscape, now in the Mauritshuis, are traditionally regarded as the earliest example of independent landscape painting in Netherlandish art. Nevertheless, for an understanding of these paintings in their true context, it is essential to know that they were created for an altarpiece that announces the salvation of mankind (cat. 1). The temporary reunification of the *Forest Scene* with the triptych from New York's Metropolitan Museum of Art arose from a desire to understand the original function and meaning of the work. This exhibition offers visitors to the Mauritshuis the unique opportunity of studying the widely-known panels showing the wooded landscape in their original setting as the outside wings of a medieval triptych.

1 Karel van Mander, *Het schilder-boeck,* Haarlem 1604, fol. 206r. Van Mander/Miedema 1994-96, I, pp. 82-83; II, pp. 265-66.
2 Friedländer 1967-76, V (1969), no. 6a-b
3 In the following summary outline of the development of the altarpiece, the below-mentioned literature was consulted: Braun 1924; Neilsen Blum 1969; Jacobs 1986; Harbison 1990; Van Os 1990; H. Nieuwdorp in Antwerp 1993, pp. 14-23; Laemers 1995; See also Edwin Buijsen's article in this catalogue, in particular pp. 28-31.
4 Van Oudheusden 1988, p. 52; see also the article by Edwin Buijsen in this catalogue, note 15.
5 Laemers 1995, no. 244, p. 2, note 3.
6 Ehresmann 1982, especially pp. 359-60, fig. 2.

Celebrating the reunification of Gerard David's triptych

Yvette Bruijnen

For many years Gerard David's wings with a wooded landscape have adorned the walls of the Mauritshuis. Originally, however, these paintings formed part of a triptych now owned by the Metropolitan Museum of Art in New York (figs 1 and 2). Of this superb triptych the panels in The Hague form the exterior of the wings. At some time in the past these wings were sawn apart so that the scenes on the two sides became separated from each other. After a turbulent history this triptych by Gerard David (c.1450-1523) can once more be seen in its original form.

The centre panel shows the Nativity taking place in a ruin. Mary and Joseph are kneeling at the manger, worshipping the Child; in front of it is a basket with swaddling clothes, a sheaf of wheat and a staff. Behind the manger the ox and ass are lying and in the top left corner a group of angels is in full flight clad in elegant and colourful garments. Through a gap in the wall one can glimpse the shepherds and their flock with an angel bringing them the news of the birth of the Redeemer. Two of the shepherds have already arrived at the ruin and are gazing over the wall at the scene.

The wings show the two donors of the triptych worshipping the new born Child. The woman is wearing a gown with a splendid brocade pattern and precious jewels. The couple are accompanied by two saints. Behind the man we see St Jerome in cardinal's garb with his lion. This creature followed the saint everywhere after he had drawn a thorn from its paw.[1] Standing behind the female donor is a saint who was formerly identified as St Vincent, who usually holds a gridiron.[2] We now know that it is in fact St Leonard. With some difficulty we can recognize the object he is holding in his left hand as a manacle; this was St Leonard's usual attribute as patron saint of prisoners.[3]

The donors themselves are also provided with the attributes of different saints. The man is accompanied by St Anthony's attribute, a pig. Pig's fat was traditionally used as a remedy for St Anthony's fire (erysipelas), an eleventh century epidemic during which, legend had it that, many of the sufferers were healed by the saint.[4] The woman has the crown, wheel and sword of St Catherine, attributes of her royal status and martyrdom. These attributes were probably added as references of the names of the donors.[5] In their closed state the two scenes on the reverse of the wings show a continuous wooded landscape without any human figures. In the wood one can see a building and a few animals. The two animals in the right-hand wing close to the water are often described in the literature as two oxen;[6] in fact, they are an ox and an ass. There is also an ass in the left-hand wing.

The scenes, executed in oil paint, show a great technical refinement. David has produced subtle graduations of colours by using transparent glazes. The precision of the execution is evident in the details, such as the still life in the foreground of the centre panel. A very felicitous feature is the rendering of the loose spiky straws that have fallen from the manger and the wheatsheaf. The rope tied round the horns of the ox is almost tangible. The ruin consists of dilapidated walls with crumbling stones on which small plants are growing. The plant on the wall above the ox and the ass is painted so realistically that one can see straightaway that it is a dandelion.

The trees and plants in the *Forest Scene* are meticulously painted and very lifelike. The leaves of the three main trees are of different shapes and colours so that they can easily be identified. From left to right we see an oak, a silver walnut tree and a beech. Many of the water plants along the bank of the stream are also recognizable, such as yellow irises and the plantain.[7] The realistic treatment of the trees and plants make it seem likely that David drew studies after nature, although we only know of one sketch of a tree by him.[8]

The two halves of the wooded landscape do not join perfectly, because part of the central tree that is painted over both wings is missing. This missing part is, in a sense, compensated by the frames. The same function is fulfilled by the frames around the three sections of the scene on the interior.[9] Moreover, the architecture serves to unify the composition of the whole, with similar colours and elements occurring in all three scenes – the crumbling walls, the windows and the battlements. The different parts of the architecture function as a sort of stage set in which each figure is assigned a distinct place. The donors are depicted somewhat larger than the saints behind them. This serves to reinforce the spatial effect, since the donors are in any case closer to the viewer than are the saints. The movement suggested by the group of angels is in splendid contrast with the still devotion of the main figures. With their wind-blown garments they fly downward towards the Christ Child. Since the angels in the foreground are somewhat larger than those behind them, they also add to the spatial effect.

The space depicted in the *Forest Scene* is more closed in character. The trees that cover almost the entire surface of the painting leave only a small area of sky free. David has deliberately limited the range of the viewer's gaze, thus giving one the feeling of being in the wood oneself.

THE PLACE IN DAVID'S ŒUVRE

Only a few of David's paintings, drawings or miniatures are dated. The precise place of the triptych in his œuvre is thus difficult to determine. There is general agreement however that the triptych described here belongs to his later period.[10] In 1484 Gerard David, who originally came from Oudewater (near Gouda), established himself in Bruges as a master painter, continuing a flourishing practice there until his death in 1523.[11] The datable paintings all come from this period. In 1498 for instance he had completed two ambitious paintings with scenes of the judgement of Cambyses (Groeningemuseum, Bruges) and in 1509 he donated his *Virgo inter Virgines* to the Convent of Sion in Bruges (Musée des Beaux-Arts, Rouen).[12] His altarpiece with the Baptism of Christ can be dated to between 1502 and 1508 on the basis of the biographical data of the donors of this triptych (fig. 3).[13] The latter work illustrates the fact that landscape played an important role in David's later work. The *Forest Scene* on the Mauritshuis panels can be regarded as David's supreme achievement in the depiction of landscape. For the first time human figures are entirely absent from his landscape scene. This is not only an exception in his work but is also unique for this period. Seen in conjunction with the advanced depiction of spatial effects in the scenes on the inside, it would argue for a late dating of the triptych, between 1505 and 1515.

In this relatively late period the influence of the work of the Ghent painter, Hugo van der Goes (1440-1482), can still be discerned – a painter whose presence can also be felt in other paintings by David.[14] Some important elements of the composition described here, such as the manger with Mary and Joseph kneeling in adoration, also occur in Van der Goes' famous painting of *The Nativity* (fig. 4).[15]

AN EVENTFUL HISTORY

The earliest known owner of the triptych was Ramon F. Urrutia of Madrid in around 1920. At that time the triptych was still intact. It is said that it had already belonged for some centuries to this family that originally came from Navarra in Spain.[16] The triptych passed from the Urrutia family to the well-known art dealer Joseph Duveen in Paris and New York who sold it in 1928 to the collector Jules S. Bache in New York.[17] Bache loaned his collection of paintings to the Metropolitan Museum of Art in 1943, after which David's triptych was bequeathed

to the museum in 1949.[18] Earlier on however, between 1930 and 1932, the scenes on the reverse of the wings were sawn off and returned to Duveen.[19] The reason for this drastic treatment was probably the conviction current at the time that the landscape was not painted by David.[20] A photo of the *Forest Scene* from the 1920s shows why it was not regarded as original: the building was overpainted in curious fashion with details that were intended to be 'picturesque' (fig. 5).[21] Nevertheless, in 1932 the Rijksmuseum in Amsterdam bought the wings as Gerard David's work.[22] The restoration carried out prior to the purchase must certainly have contributed to this rehabilitation. The 'picturesque' overpainting of the cottage was removed and replaced with a new overpainting, integrating the house, convincingly this time, with the whole composition (fig. 6).[23] Since then doubt has no longer been cast on the attribution to David. In 1948 the outside wings passed as a long-term loan to the Mauritshuis where they remain to this day.

The history of the triptych has clearly shown that it has had a great deal to endure. After the outside wings were sawn off, the original wooden supports of the triptych were removed in New York and the paintings were transferred to canvas.[24] This treatment caused the loss of parts of the ground and underdrawing, something that has been confirmed by infrared reflectography.[25] The surface structure of the paint was changed by the transfer to canvas so that the luminosity and vividness of the colours were seriously affected. In addition, the upper layers of the glaze became worn. The modelling of the faces of the donors is largely lost, which has resulted in their austere appearance. While the figure of Mary in the centre panel has been reasonably well preserved, the contrast between the two different shades of blue of her dress and robe has

1 *Gerard David,* Triptych with the Nativity, Donors, and Saints Jerome and Leonard. *Panels transferred onto canvas, 90.2 × 71.1 cm (centre piece) and 90.2 × 31.4 cm (wings). The Metropolitan Museum of Art, New York, The Jules S. Bache Collection, 1949.*

2 *Gerard David*, Forest Scene.
*Outer wings, 30.7 × 89.9 cm
(each). Mauritshuis, The Hague
(on loan from the Rijksmuseum,
Amsterdam).*

3 *Gerard David*, Baptism of
Christ. *Panel, 132 × 96.6 cm
(centre panel) and 132.2 × 42.2 cm
(wings). Groeningemuseum,
Bruges.*

4 *Hugo van der Goes*, Nativity.
*Panel, 97 × 245 cm. Staatliche
Museen Preussischer Kulturbesitz,
Gemäldegalerie, Berlin. (p. 17)*

largely disappeared.[26] The rich nuances of colour of the wings and garments of the angels must also once have been breathtaking; their hues are now less intense due to abrasion. In the background of the centre panel one can see blue underpainting in some places.

The restoration of the *Forest Scene*

The wafer-thin sawn-off outside wings were fortunately not transferred to canvas but were glued onto new wooden supports to strengthen them. The paint has as a result retained more of its original surface structure, than is the case with the triptych in New York. However, in 1985 the *Forest Scene* had to be restored.[27] Not only did a thick dark layer of varnish obscure the original colours; during the last restoration prior to the purchase by the Rijksmuseum, the landscape in the foreground of the left wing had largely been overpainted.[28] After the removal of this overpainting, the condition of the panel became more evident. It could be seen that little remained of the original paint layer depicting the house. During the earlier

restoration no attention had been paid to incorporate these original fragments in the overpainting. By the entrance gate for instance, the higher central section with the turrets had been painted out and replaced with two windows. The building moreover ended up as a water mill due to the narrow path being converted into a stream. The house was again retouched in the restoration of 1985, with the traces of the original paint now being taken into account.

The reconstruction of the house was made easier through the good fortune that a painting with a similar wooded landscape has been preserved (fig. 7). This painting in Genoa is attributed to Ambrosius Benson (?-1550) and depicts the rest on the flight into Egypt.[29] Comparison of the two houses has made it possible to solve a number of uncertainties about David's painting (figs 8 and 9). It became clear, for instance, that not one but two dormer windows were painted in the sloping roof, just as in the painting in Genoa. Also the function of the bulge under the eaves of the tower on the left hand

5 *Gerard David*, Forest Scene
(state before 1932, photo, Max J.
Friedländer archive, Netherlands
Institute for Art History,
The Hague).

6 *Gerard David*, Forest Scene
(state between 1932 and 1985).

7 *Attributed to Ambrosius
Benson*, Rest on the Flight into
Egypt. *Panel, 61 × 53 cm. Galleria
Durazzo-Pallavicini, Genoa.*

8 *Attributed to Ambrosius
Benson*, Rest on the Flight into
Egypt *(detail of fig. 7).*

9 *Gerard David*, Forest Scene
(detail of left wing).

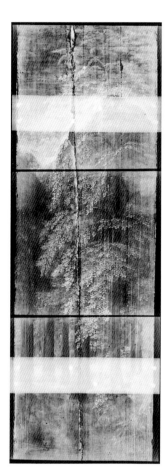

*10 Gerard David, Forest Scene
(photograph of the X-radiographs).*

side became clear: it was an earthenware pot where doves were kept, as we can see from the numerous white birds circling round the tower in the panel in Genoa.

REST ON THE FLIGHT INTO EGYPT

Benson, a painter from Bruges, was active in David's studio for a number of years. Art historians have used Benson's œuvre as a veritable repository, attributing to him any number of paintings that bear some stylistic resemblance to the work of Gerard David.[30] A certain caution is appropriate then in attributing the *Rest on the Flight into Egypt* to him. It is clear however that it was painted by an artist in David's circle, but one who used a different, more simple painting technique than did the master. The gradations of colour in the leaves for instance are not produced with transparent glazes, but by juxtaposing light and dark brush strokes. At a distance they seem to blend. This painting treatment would suggest that the work is of a later period than David's *Forest Scene*.

The painter of the *Rest on the Flight into Egypt* has brought the wooded landscape together in a single panel. In the centre, however, the large tree is depicted in its entirety and a religious episode has been incorporated in the composition, with Mary, Joseph and the Child and some background figures. The scene has moreover been extended below, with additions such as Mary's robes, the basket with swaddling clothes and the prominent fern in the bottom right corner. The recumbent ass in the *Forest Scene* is replaced by that of Mary and Joseph which is proportionally larger. The ox and ass by the water have been omitted, as has the bush with the great tit.

Although the foliage of the trees corresponds in detail to that of the *Forest Scene*, it is also different in parts. The tree on the extreme left has more open areas than in David's painting where the leaves form an impenetrable screen, blocking out the sky. The X-radiographs of the *Forest Scene*, however, shows that David had initially painted more sky there (fig. 10). In the first paint layer he had indicated the sky with a light colour, using plenty of lead white. Because this white pigment easily absorbs X-rays, the area looks whitish in the X-radiographs. Probably, the painter's initial idea was to show more of the sky through the foliage. However, while he was painting David decided to cover the sky on the left almost entirely with leaves. The X-radiographs suggest that the *Forest Scene* and the *Rest on the Flight into Egypt* could well have had a model in common. It was not unusual at the time for painters to draw on each other's compositions.[31] An archival document dated 1519 shows that David, Benson and Adriaen Isenbrant (?-1551), himself a follower of David, even exchanged model drawings.[32] The model drawing of the wooded landscape probably included more sky, especially in the green of the tree on the left. In that case David followed the example in his first design, but later made a deliberate decision to change it. The painter of the *Rest on the Flight into Egypt* must have followed the model more exactly. This hypothetical model drawing must have been fairly detailed, given the resemblance between the different paintings in their treatment of the foliage areas and of the light.

The lack of human figures has often led to the *Forest Scene* being praised as the first autonomous landscape painting in Netherlandish art. In terms of its content, however, the landscape is intimately related to the relgious scene on the inside of the triptych. The following article explores in depth the meaning of David's scenes.

I am grateful to Edwin Buijsen, whose research was fundamental to this contribution. I would also like to thank Maryan Ainsworth for putting the results of her research at my disposal. At the Mauritshuis Ariane van Suchtelen, Jørgen Wadum, Carol Pottasch and André Jordaan have all been of great assistance and have offered many useful suggestions.

1 Hall 1979, p. 169.

2 In the first publication on the triptych the saint was hypothetically identified as St Vincent (Mayer 1920, p. 97), an opinion that has been concurred with until the present. It even led later to the assumption that the donors must have been Spanish in origin since the cult of St Vincent was particularly popular in Southern Europe (L. Campbell, unpublished article of 1981, Files of the European Paintings Department, The Metropolitan Museum of Art, New York). Although we may now ignore this assumption because of the identification of St Leonard, it is noticeable that the clothing of the donor is not wholly compatible with the Flemish fashions of the time. Her wimple, decollete and jewellery are Flemish, but the gown with its wide sleeves and elaborate brocade pattern are both unusual and inordinately rich for a middle-class woman (I thank M. Madou for this information)

3 For St Leonard see: Kirschbaum/Braunfels 1968-76, VII (1974), pp. 394-98; Réau 1955-59, III (1958), pp. 799-802.

4 Hall 1979, pp. 21-22.

5 Heller 1976, p. 186; Van Miegroet 1989, p. 300. It was assumed that these attributes are later additions (L. Campbell 1981, see note 2; Bauman 1986, p. 29). However, recent X-ray research has revealed that the attributes form part of the original composition. There is an underpainting for the wheel, and it originally had one spoke broken. Study under a microscope also showed that one of the plants has been painted on top of the pig. The attributes have been considerably retouched (my thanks to M. Ainsworth for this information from her very recent research).

6 See for instance: The Hague 1945, no. 47; Haverkamp Begemann/Chong 1985, p. 58; Genaille 1986, p. 68; Van Miegroet 1989, p. 232.

7 I am grateful to Anja Buijsen for identifying the trees and plants.

8 Study of a man's head and a tree (verso), black chalk (?) on prepared paper, Kunsthalle, Hamburg (Van Miegroet 1989, no. 77).

9 It is possible that the original frames were wider, whereby the panels stood further apart. However, several writers hold the opinion that the separate parts of this composition do not fit together very well, see Scillia 1975, p. 239; Van Miegroet 1989, p. 232.

10 See for instance: Mayer 1920, p. 97; Friedländer 1924-37, VI (1928), p. 143; cat. Duveen 1941 (c.1497); The Hague 1945, no. 47; Boon 1946, p. 51 (after 1509); Cuttler 1968, p. 197; Snyder 1985, p. 191 (c.1515-1520); Van Miegroet 1989, p. 300 (c.1510-1515); Harbison 1995, p. 138 (c.1505-1510).

11 For Gerard David's biography, see Van Miegroet 1989, pp. 19-34.

12 Judgement of Cambyses, Van Miegroet 1989, no. 19. Virgo inter Virgines, Van Miegroet 1989, no. 29.

13 Van Miegroet 1989, no. 23.

14 See for instance: Mayer 1920, p. 97; Antwerp 1930, p. 35; cat. Duveen 1941; Larsen 1960, pp. 80-81, 125-26; Winkler 1964, p. 152, note 4; Cuttler 1968, p. 197; Lane 1975, p. 485; Bauman 1986, p. 30; Van Miegroet 1989, p. 300; Harbison 1995, p. 137. For the influence of the work of Hugo van der Goes on Gerard David, see also Ainsworth 1990, pp. 649-50.

15 Cat. Berlin 1975, p. 177.

16 Mayer 1920, p. 97.

17 Cat. Bache 1929, n.p., with fig.

18 Wehle 1943, p. 288; Wehle/Salinger 1947, pp. 95-96; Baetjer 1995, p. 260.

19 In 1930 the wings were still intact (Antwerp 1930, pp. 33-34, no. 95). In 1932 the outside scenes on the wings were apparently removed (Jaarverslag Rijksmuseum (Annual Report) 1932, p. 8).

20 Mayer 1920, p. 97; Antwerp 1930, p. 36.

21 Friedländer wrote on the reverse of the photograph that he saw the triptych on 17 April 1928.

22 The purchase price of the outside scenes of the wings with the wooded landscape was 10,000 guilders (Rijksmuseum Archives, Amsterdam). On 17 December 1932 the wings arrived in the Rijksmuseum. The left wing was donated by the Photo Commission (paid for out of the revenues from the Rembrandt exhibition), while the right wing was bought by the State (with thanks to Annemarie Geerts, Rijksmuseum, Amsterdam). See also: Jaarverslag Rijksmuseum (Annual Report) 1932, p. 8; Luijten 1984, p. 384, 421. In Van Thiel et al. 1976, p. 189 and Sluijter-Seijffert et al. 1993, p. 51, 1942 is erroneously stated as the date of purchase.

23 Duveen's invoice for the sale to the Rijksmuseum of the Forest Scene states that the left wing was restored during his ownership (Photo Commission Archive, inv.no. 66).

24 Friedländer 1924-37, XIV (1937) is the first to point this out, p. 106.

25 Only a few fragments of the underdrawing can be seen (thanks to M. Ainsworth for this information).

26 An example of well-preserved, contrasting blues in Mary's attire can be seen in David's *Rest on the Flight into Egypt*, see p. 36, fig. 8.

27 The restoration was completed in 1987. The report and photo documentation of the restoration can be found in the files of the Mauritshuis.

28 The meadow with the ass in the left wing was also overpainted. This was why doubt was cast on the originality of the animal. To investigate this Prof. J.R.J. van Asperen de Boer took paint samples in the ass and the meadow, of which he prepared paint cross-sections. This proved that the ass was indeed original. The animal was painted on top of the green underpainting in a single paint layer. Round the ass a layer of green glaze has been applied on top of the underpainting for the meadow.

29 I thank the Marchioness Cattaneo Adorno for her friendly assistance in this matter and for her permission to reproduce this painting.
See for this painting: Marlier 1957, pp. 88-89, 124; Friedländer 1967-76, XI (1974), no. 246; Ragghianti 1990, p. 213, no. 419.
In the Hermitage in St Petersburg there is a variation on the centre panel of David's triptych showing the Nativity. This painting has also been attributed to Benson, see Nikulin 1989, p. 36.

30 The same is also the case with Adriaen Isenbrant, to whom no less than five hundred paintings have been attributed (see: Wilson 1995, pp. 1-17).

31 Wilson 1995, p. 4.

32 Van Miegroet 1989, p. 344.

Considering the Ox and the Ass
In search of an interpretation for
Gerard David's *Forest Scene*

Edwin Buijsen

For generations art historians have been intrigued by the painting showing a mysterious wooded landscape that decorates the outside of the wings of Gerard David's triptych, now in the Mauritshuis. It fascinates not only because of its totally convincing representation of nature, but also because of the complete absence of human figures (p. 15, in colour). The picture consists chiefly of tall trees, whose thick foliage creates an almost impenetrable screen. Only a few animals disturb the serene silence of these woods: on the right-hand wing an ox and an ass are seen wading in a shallow pool, while on the left a second donkey is resting on a small hill and a great tit has alighted upon what resembles a blackberry bush. A winding road leads towards a somewhat unusual building with a tower and gateway, which provide the sole trace of human presence in an otherwise untouched natural setting.

In art-historical literature this scene is frequently cited as the earliest example of an independent landscape painting in Netherlandish art.[1] Until then, the representation of landscape was limited to backgrounds in religious pictures and portraits (see cat. 2). Even in the work of David's contemporary, Joachim Patinir (*c.*1485-1524), who may be considered the first specialist in this area, the landscape is still peopled with religious or mythological staffage.[2] Not until the close of the sixteenth century did the art of landscape painting develop into an independent genre that was to reach its zenith in the following century with the work of such masters as Jan van Goyen (1596-1656) and Jacob van Ruisdael (1628/29-1682).

Although apparently lacking a deliberate subject, it seems at the least somewhat contentious to apply the term 'independent landscape' to the forest scene in the Mauritshuis. After all, the picture was not planned as an independent piece but originally formed part of a larger composition with a distinctly religious meaning. Thus we should not consider the landscape without including the inside of the triptych which depicts the Nativity of Christ being witnessed by the donors and certain saints (p. 14, in colour). The remarkable nature of this event is clearly presented on the centre panel, in numerous details.[3] The sheaf of corn in the foreground right refers not only to the meaning in Hebrew of the word Bethlehem (House of Bread) but also to Christ as the Bread of Life. The eye-catching position of the basket containing swaddling bands may be interpreted as a call to the viewer to greet

1 Jan Gossaert, Adam and Eve in the Garden of Eden. *Outside wings of a triptych. Panel, 45 × 17.5 cm (each). Galleria Nazionale, Palermo.*

2 *Gerard David,* Annunciation.
Outside wings of a triptych.
Panel, 86.4 × 28 cm (each).
The Metropolitan Museum of Art,
New York, Robert Lehman
Collection.

the Christ Child with feelings of motherly tenderness and care. In fifteenth-century devotional writings we find an elaborate description of how the believer should spiritually wash and clothe the newborn Child.[4] In the background a dandelion can be seen growing on a brick wall, an unusual place for such a plant. This weed, which flowered during the period when Easter is celebrated, was taken as a reminder of the Passion of Christ.[5] It is as if the painter, by placing the dandelion immediately above the newborn Child, is making a reference to Christ's sacrificial death on the Cross. Finally, the dilapidated building which serves as a backdrop for the religious scene quite likely refers to the palace of the Old Testament king David. This is a reference to the Old Covenant between God and the Jewish people which is now replaced by the New Covenant, through the coming of the Redeemer.[6]

Although the scene on the centre panel is replete with symbols from Christianity, the two outside wings appear not to contain any easily recognisable references to the history of the redemption. Nevertheless, several writers have tried to probe the deeper significance of this wooded landscape. Shortly after the re-discovery of the triptych, Max J. Friedländer – an expert in early Netherlandish art – suggested that originally the figures of Adam and Eve were presented on the outside wings, but were overpainted at a later date.[7] That the father and mother of mankind should appear on the outside of a triptych presenting the birth of Christ seems in many ways most appropriate. The burden of sin placed on mankind by Adam and Eve came to an end with the coming of Christ and his death on the cross. Indeed, Christ and Mary were seen as the second Adam and Eve.[8] There are several triptychs from the early sixteenth century that show on the outside a paradisiacal landscape with Adam and Eve, including the so-called Malvagna triptych (fig. 1) by Jan Gossaert (c.1478-1532).[9] However, even after its most recent restoration the outside of the David triptych shows not a trace of a human figure, nor do we find the great variety of animals which traditionally inhabit the earthly Paradise.[10]

Among the very few creatures in this woodland scene, we see an ox and two donkeys. Various writers have recognised here the well-known animals from the Nativity scene who occupy so prominent a position on the centre panel of this triptych. It has even been suggested by some that the building on the left-hand wing could be the inn where there was no room for Joseph and Mary to stay.[11] In 1990 Esther Cleven undertook a more thorough analysis.[12] Because the scene contains certain elements that also occur in depictions of the rest on the flight to Egypt – such as the donkey and the woodland setting – she considered this to be the theme of David's *Forest Scene*. The fact that the main actors in this story are omitted was, she argued, because they could not be suitably presented on the two outside wings. If they were painted in the centre of the picture, they would be, as it were, cut through the middle when the two wings were closed. Were they to be painted on only one wing, this would disturb the balance of the composition. Cleven maintained that the sixteenth-century viewer, familiar with pictures of the rest on the flight to Egypt, would have sufficient indications from such slight references as the ox and the ass to recall the rest of the story. All the more so since the figures of Joseph, Mary and the Infant Christ were displayed large and clear on the inside of the centre panel.

A totally different interpretation was suggested in 1995 by Ursula Härting.[13] She proposed a connection between the ox and ass in David's *Forest Scene* and a text from the biblical Book of Job which describes how God's majesty is displayed through nature. In this passage God poses Job various questions, including the ones: 'Who hath sent out the wild ass free? Or who hath loosed the bands of the wild ass? Whose house I have made the wilderness, and the barren land his dwellings?' (Job 39:5-6), and 'Does the wild ox consent to serve you, does it spend the night in your stall?' (Job 39:9). The answer to these rhetorical questions can only be that the animals are subject to no authority but that of God. Härting suggests that the outside wings of David's triptych show the wild ass and the forest ox roaming in an unspoilt natural setting, before they became subject to any master; in contrast, on the centre panel they are shown docilely kneeling before the newborn Child and thereby recognising God as their Lord. Härting considered this balance of question and answer (as in the Book of Job) to be the linking element between the inside and outside paintings on this triptych.

Every attempt to interpret David's *Forest Scene* is complicated by the fact that we are dealing here with a unique work. As far as is known there is no other triptych with a comparable representation on the outside of the wings. This means that art historians cannot base their investigations on an extensive pictorial tradition but must deal with incidental factors which are difficult to establish. For example, the wishes of the donor may have played a role, as well as the place where the triptych was to stand, and its purpose. In this case, we have no information regarding these points and we are therefore thrown back upon general reflections concerning the original function of a triptych.[14] Triptychs of this sort were usually intended to be placed on the altar in a church or chapel.[15] To judge from the size of David's triptych, which is fairly modest in comparison with other altarpieces, it was not intended to stand on a high altar. More probably it was made for a side chapel or perhaps even an altar in a house chapel. It would seem most credible that an altarpiece would be set in a place that belonged to the donors, or to an official body that was supported or sponsored by them. So far we have no clues about the identity of the donors whom we see portrayed on the inside of the wings. Thus we can only guess at the motives which inspired the commissioning of this work.

Generally speaking, this type of religious foundation was prompted by the desire for personal salvation. By setting up an altar people not only demonstrated their own piety but also created a place where Mass could be celebrated until the end of time and prayers said to ensure that after death their souls would ascend into heaven. A priest could be employed specially to say Mass in the chapel on certain days. That this was considered of great importance is shown by a document that refers to another work by Gerard David, the triptych illustrating the baptism of Christ (p. 16, fig. 3).[16] After the death of the patron, Jan des Trompes, a dignitary from Bruges, his heirs donated the triptych to the Brotherhood of the Sworn Clerks of the Bruges tribunal (the confraternity of lawyers), to be placed in their chapel in the church of St Basil (which was the lower church in the basilica of the Sacred Blood). In return the Brotherhood was to celebrate a solemn requiem mass every year in the chapel on 10 December. Furthermore, it had to be promised that Mass would be celebrated on the saints' days of James and Christopher, the patron saints of Des Trompes' third wife, and of her new husband. After their deaths requiem masses would be recited. To ensure that the Brotherhood

3 Gerard David, Nativity of
Christ. *Panel, 85.2 × 57.5 cm.*
Museum of Art, Cleveland (Ohio).

4 *Gerard David,* Forest Scene
(detail of left wing).

5 *Gerard David,* Forest Scene
(detail of left wing).

6 *Gerard David,* Forest Scene
(detail of right wing).

continued these observances the heirs placed a memorial plaque in the wall beside the altar on which were inscribed the conditions stipulating the donation of the altarpiece. If these conditions were not met, first of all a fine was imposed and finally the altarpiece was to be returned to the family.

It is possible that David's triptych showing the birth of Christ likewise graced an altar where Mass was said in memory of the donors and their families. By opening or closing the wings of the triptych the picture seen upon the altar could be varied. As far as is known there were no fixed rules regarding the opening and shutting of triptychs. Presumably they were opened on Sundays and festivals and probably also during Mass on weekdays. In some churches the altarpieces remained symbolically shut during Lent and Advent, the two main penitential periods in the church calendar.[17]

The difference between a closed and an open triptych is usually emphasised by the sober representation on the outside of the wings. It is not unusual for the painting to be a grisaille, a technique using only grey tones and often creating the effect of unpolychromed three-dimensionality. This produces a strong contrast with the colourful interior.[18] But even when it has more colour the outside tends to be restrained in its presentation.

If a list is drawn up of the subject matter on the outside of wings we find that the Annunciation – the message of the angel to the Virgin Mary announcing the birth of Christ – is by far the most common, particularly so when the inside of the triptych presents scenes from the life of Christ or the Virgin Mary (fig. 2).[19] The Annunciation stands at the beginning of the story of mankind's redemption which culminates in Christ's sacrificial death and resurrection. Thus this theme, pre-sented on the outside of the wings, introduces the scenes that will be revealed once the triptych is opened. Another popular subject depicted on outer wings – Adam and Eve (fig. 1) – can also be interpreted as a proclamation of the coming of the Saviour. The same holds for prophets and Sibyls who announced the coming of Christ. In all these instances there is a strong relationship between the outside and inside of the triptych, which becomes apparent when the wings are successively closed and opened.

In the cases where there is no such relationship, the outside of the triptych generally presents something directly connected with the donors such as their patron saints or their family coats of arms.[20] In the case of the above-mentioned triptych showing the baptism of Christ, the outer wings include a portrait of Jan des Trompes' second wife, Magdalena Cordier, who is kneeling in front of the Virgin Mary and the Christ Child accompanied by her holy namesake and a daughter. The fact that she is portrayed on the outside of the triptych can be easily explained by the fact that the donor's first wife and children already occupied the inside.

Since the wooded landscape on the wings in the Mauritshuis apparently contains no obvious references to the donors it is possible that the scene acts in the same way as the Annunciation, as a proclamation of the birth of Christ – which will become apparent when the wings are unfolded. If this is so, there should be a connection between the scenes on the outside and inside. The most obvious link is the presence of the ox and the ass on both outer wings and the centre panel. Indeed, the two animals are so placed on the central panel that when the wings are opened, they immediately spring into view. Also when we compare this presentation with others of the same theme – including some by David himself – it is remarkable how important is the position given here to these two creatures (fig. 3).[21] The ox and the ass kneel beside the manger and warm the naked baby with breath from their nostrils. This type of representation can be compared with the description of Christ's birth in the *Meditationes Vitae Christi,* a popular devotional writing from the late Middle Ages. In a Middle Dutch translation of this text, found in a manuscript from Bruges dated to 1487, we read how Mary laid the Child in a manger beside the ox and ass who 'breathed and blew upon him that they might warm his blessed tiny frail body, as if they recognised him and understood his need, for it was bitter cold.'[22]

The presence of the ox and ass at the birth of Christ – incidentally not mentioned in the Gospels – goes back to a tradition far older than the *Meditationes,* based on the first Christian writers.[23] The earliest mention of an ox and an ass at the birth of Christ is by Origenes in the third century. In it he found the fulfilment of the words of the prophet Isaiah, 'The ox knoweth his owner, and the ass his master's crib' (Isaiah 1:3).[24] The ox as a clean animal symbolised for him the people of Israel while the donkey stood for the impure heathen. In the fourth century this allegory was further elaborated by Gregory of Nyssa who wrote that the ox is bound by the Jewish law and the ass bears the burden of idolatry, while between them lies the Christ Child who will free both groups from their yokes of bondage.[25] Numerous other writers described the ox and ass beside the manger and it was not long before the two animals became an inextricable part of the Christmas story.[26] In the pseudo-Gospel of Matthew, an apocryphal book widely read in the Middle Ages, we find 'And the ox and the ass worshipped Him. Thus the words of the prophet Isaiah were fulfilled.'[27]

The question remains what the ox and ass at the birth of Christ – seen in this context as symbolising mankind before the coming of the Saviour – have to do with the animals on the outside of David's triptych. A possible explanation lies in the writings of the church father St Jerome (*c*.347-420), whose person and works both enjoyed a renewed popularity in the early sixteenth century.[28] There are many occasions where Jerome proclaims himself an ardent supporter of the notion of Origenes that the presence of ox and ass at the crib of Christ represents the fulfilment of the words of Isaiah cited above.[29] In his commentary on Isaiah he connected this passage with another text from the prophet which refers to the same animals: 'Blessed are ye that sow beside all waters, that send forth thither the feet of the ox and the ass' (Isaiah 32:20).[30] This line occurs at the end of a Messianic prophecy about the establishment of the kingdom of peace and righteousness, in which the prophet calls for repentance before God's rule can hold sway (Isaiah 32:9-20).

This passage describes how untroubled days will be followed by a period of disasters when the harvest will fail, the ground produce only weeds and the city be deserted. This will come to an end when the spirit of the Messiah is poured out over the earth, and justice and righteousness will flourish:

Tremble ye women that are at ease; be troubled, ye careless ones; strip you and make you bare and gird sackcloth upon your loins. And beat your breasts for the pleasant fields, for the fruitful vine. Upon the land of my people shall come up thorns and briars; yea, upon all the houses of joy in the joyous city; Because the palaces shall be forsaken, the multitude of the city shall be left; the forts and towers shall be dens forever, a joy of wild asses, a pasture of flocks; Until the spirit be poured upon us from on high and the wilderness be a fruitful field and the fruitful field be counted for a forest. Then judgement shall dwell in the wilderness and righteousness in the fruitful field. And the work of righteousness shall be peace; and the effect of righteousness quietness and assurance forever. And my people shall dwell in a peaceable habitation, and in sure dwellings and in quiet resting places; When it shall hail, coming down on the forest; and the city shall be low in a low place. Blessed are ye that sow beside all waters, that send forth thither the feet of the ox and the ass (Isaiah 32:11-20).[31]

When we read this text carefully we find remarkable parallels with David's *Forest Scene*. First, there is the 'forest' that occupies so prominent a position on the two wings of the triptych. Then there are the words of the prophet describing how 'the multitude of the city shall be left' which appears to match the total absence of human figures in David's representation. The bush resembling a bramble that occupies the left foreground may be linked with the 'thorns and briars' that fill the fields, while the donkey resting in the picture is possibly a reference to the 'wild asses' that now inhabit the desolate country (fig. 4). The building in the background may well be one of the 'houses of joy' that now stands deserted (fig. 5).[32] Finally, on the right-hand wing the ox and the ass beside the water match the closing sentence of the passage, 'Blessed are ye that sow beside all waters, that send forth thither the feet of the ox and the ass' (fig. 6).

Based on this text from Isaiah, David's *Forest Scene* can be interpreted as the envisioning of a prophecy that

foretells the coming of the Saviour. Seen this way, the scene on the outside of the wings forms a prelude to the inside of the triptych where the words of the prophet are fulfilled through the birth of Christ.

As I have already mentioned, Ursula Härting explained the panels in the Mauritshuis by means of a passage in the Book of Job. However, although it is not excluded that contemporary viewers also connected the scene with this biblical passage, in itself the text contains too few links to assume that it is the basis for the *Forest Scene*. Furthermore, the story of Christ's nativity bears far less reference to the Book of Job than to the prophecies of Isaiah. After all, the ox and ass beside the crib are taken from this source.

The words of Isaiah, who was seen as one of the major Old Testament prophets, held an important place in the liturgy connected with Christmas. In order to show how the life of Christ fulfilled the Messianic prophecies in the Old Testament, passages from Isaiah were – and are to this day – read during the Christmas church services.[33] These readings would begin during the Advent period that leads up to Christmas, when Christian believers contemplate the longing for the Messiah's coming as expressed in the Old Testament, and place this in the context of the birth of Christ.

Possibly the passage from Isaiah cited above, in which the Messianic kingdom is described as a forest where ox and ass wander freely, may have been read aloud at the Christmas season in the chapel where this triptych by David stood displayed. Although today this particular text from Isaiah is read during Advent we so far have no information about when it was read in the late fifteenth and early sixteenth century. We do know that the passage was not one of the most loved prophecies from Isaiah relating to the birth of the Messiah. You may search in vain for this text in popular devotional literature, while other passages from Isaiah are frequently cited.[34]

However, the lack of a strong liturgical or literary tradition does not necessarily indicate that the interpretation of David's *Forest Scene* as proposed here need be summarily dismissed. As already mentioned, this is an exceptional case probably determined by the personal choice of the donor. Nor is it out of the question that a scholarly friend or acquaintance in holy orders may have brought the text from Isaiah to the donor's attention, and indeed given instructions to the painter.[35]

It was recently pointed out by Craig Harbison that in the fifteenth and sixteenth century altarpieces answered a need for 'a novelistic and personal form of visual expression.'[36] Since they were frequently placed in the intimacy of a private chapel, the representation on the panels only needed to be understood by a small initiated group. A fine example of this is a triptych by Hans Memling, the outside of which depicts a highly unusual scene showing cranes in a landscape (fig. 7). Not until the donor was identified as the Italian archbishop Benedetto Pagagnotti was the explanation for these creatures found. In classical antiquity the common crane was named *grus vigilans* because of its supposed watchfulness, or vigilance. The Latin *vigilans* translated the Greek *episcopos* (which means in English 'he who watches over') and is the Greek word used for a bishop. Seen thus, the cranes refer to the bishop's primary task, that of watching over his flock.[37] This example makes it very clear how personal choices played a decisive role in the selection of the subject matter that was displayed on an altarpiece. When, as in the case of the David triptych, the donor's identity is unknown, it is difficult to decipher the underlying motives. Nevertheless, it seems difficult to ignore the impression that in this case the donor was at least partly influenced by a great love of nature. And by employing Gerard David to paint this triptych he chose an artist who was a real expert in painting wooded landscapes.

Since David's commission was to paint a scene on the outside of the wings that had never been depicted before, it seems logical that he turned to other examples in which a forest landscape plays an important part. By far the most important of these is the *Rest on the Flight to Egypt* which David frequently portrayed (fig. 8).[38] This would explain why the forest scene in the Mauritshuis contains elements that are apparently borrowed from scenes showing the rest during the flight – as pointed out by Esther Cleven (see above). In this connection it is understandable that one of David's later followers took over the composition of the *Forest Scene* virtually unchanged and used it as the background for a painting of the rest on the flight (p. 19, fig. 7).

We do not know who commissioned this triptych showing the birth of Christ, nor where it originally stood. Thus any interpretation of the scene on the outside of the wings should be made with due caution. Nevertheless, the parallels between this wooded landscape and the cited passage from Isaiah are so striking that we may assume some connection with this text. Certain ambiguities remain, such as the presence of the great tit on the left-hand panel. This small bird also occurs in the paintings of Jerome Bosch (*c*.1450-1516) and has been interpreted as a reference to the indecisive nature of mankind, people as it were fluttering between good and evil.[39] The same small creature was seen in the Middle Ages and

7 *Hans Memling,* Cranes in a landscape. *Outside wings of a triptych. Panel, 56 × 17 cm (each). The National Gallery, London.*

8 *Gerard David*, Rest on the
Flight to Egypt. *Panel,*
50.8 × 43.2 cm. The Metropolitan
Museum of Art, New York,
Jules S. Bache Collection, 1949.

Renaissance both as a symbol of fertility, as well as of justice and truth.[40] Although it is tempting to connect this latter with the prophecy of Isaiah that 'righteousness (will remain) in the fruitful field' we cannot assert with any precision what is the meaning of the great tit in David's painting. Concluding, we may say that although the text from the prophet Isaiah brings some clarification about the meaning of David's picture, this leafy landscape has by no means disclosed all its secrets.

I would like to thank R.L. Falkenburg, M. Madou and P.H. Schrijvers for their valuable comments and suggestions.

1 See e.g.: Nieburg 1946; Van Puyvelde 1947, no. 30; Stechow 1966, p. 64; Snyder 1985, pp. 191-92; Haverkamp Begemann/Chong 1985, pp. 57-58; Devisscher 1992, p. 191 and Ridderbos 1995, pp. 123-24.
2 See Falkenburg 1988.
3 For the iconography of the Nativity of Christ, see Smits 1933, pp. 52-58 and also the literature listed in note 23 below.
4 Examples can be found in Moll 1854, II, pp. 308-09 and Axters 1950-60, III, p. 295. See also Buijsen 1986, p. 54.
5 Levi d'Ancona 1977, p. 126. For the meaning of the dandelion see also Behling 1967, pp. 33-36, 79-80.
6 On this symbolism see for example I. Vandevivere in Bruges/Louvain-la-Neuve 1985, p. 33 and Hall 1970, p. 269.
7 Friedländer 1924-37, VI (1928), p. 143, no. 160: 'aussen Landschaft, ehemals mit Adam und Eva, deren Figuren übermalt sind' (landscape, once with the figures of Adam and Eve which are now painted over).
8 Timmers 1974, p. 36; Guldan 1966 and Bröker 1995, pp. 22-26.
9 Friedländer 1967-76, VIII (1972), no. 2, pl. 6. For a further example see Friedländer 1967-76, XI (1974), no. 125, pl. 103 (Isenbrant). For outside wings depicting Adam and Eve in the œuvre of Gerard David, see Van Miegroet 1989, fig. 100.
10 Although L. Baldass (1936, p. 95) and K.G. Boon (1946, p. 51, note 1) refuted Friedländers assumption, it was recently restated without comment in a handbook on Dutch landscape art (Amsterdam/Boston/Philadelphia 1987-88, p. 16).
11 Haverkamp Begemann/Chong 1985, p. 58; Van Miegroet 1989, p. 232, p. 300, no. 30.
12 Cleven 1990.
13 Härting 1995.
14 This information on the function of triptychs is partly taken from Laemers 1995 (I thank Suzanne Laemers for her kind permission to make use of her unpublished thesis). See also Neilsen Blum 1969; Lane 1984; Harbison 1990 and Steinmetz 1993.
15 Because of the large number of dedicated altars in some churches these altars were also placed against pillars or the rood screen: Laemers 1995, pp. 155 and 162.
16 Van Miegroet 1989, pp. 185-86, 345-46, no. 47.
17 Teasdale Smith 1959; Butzkamm 1990, pp. 142-43; Laemers 1995, pp. 94-96, 166.
18 For grisaille depictions on outside wings see: Teasdale Smith 1959, pp. 50-52; Belting/Kruse 1994, pp. 60-62.
19 Laemers 1995, pp. 97-127, esp. pp. 100-01.
20 For examples of family coats of arms on the outsides of wings, see cat. 7 and 9.

21 Compare e.g. Van Miegroet 1989, figs 11, 13 and 20.

22 Cited in De Jong 1985, pp. 53-54. See also Ragusa/Green 1961, pp. 33-34.

23 Knipping 1942, pp. 17-21; Mak 1948, pp. 168-70; Ziegler 1952; De Jong 1985, pp. 41-42; Van der Laan 1990, pp. 197-99; Bröker 1995, pp. 57-58.

24 Ziegler 1952, p. 391. Besides the passage from Isaiah, Origenes and later writers added a second biblical text to explain the presence of ox and ass. The text is found in Habakuk 3:2: 'In the midst of the years thou didst make thyself known' but through a mis-translation of the Hebrew has been read as: 'Between two creatures shall he be found.'

25 Ziegler 1952, p. 391. For other, less common, interpretations of the ox and the ass, see Mak 1948, p. 170 en De Jong 1985, p. 41.

26 For the iconography of ox and ass, see Panofsky 1953, p. 470, note 1.

27 Cited in translation from De Jong 1985, p. 53; see also Knipping 1942, p. 26 (and p. 22 on the pseudo-Gospel of Matthew in general).

28 See for example Rice 1985, esp. pp. 116-36.

29 Mak 1948, pp. 169-70; Ziegler 1952, p. 393.

30 Corpus Christianorum 1963, pp. 8-9. In his exegesis over Isaiah 32:20 Jerome interprets the ox and ass as the Jews and the heathen, see also Corpus Christianorum 1963, pp. 408-10. Also when Jerome cites this passage in another context, he gives the same interpretation to the two animals, see for example Corpus Christianorum 1959, p. 344 (Commentarius in Ecclesiasten). Other early Christian writers also explain the ox and ass in Isaiah 32:20 as the Jews and the heathen before the coming of Christ, see e.g. Clemens of Alexandria, p. 233. Bonaventura had a marked preference for this verse, which he cites on several occasions in his commentary on St Luke's gospel: Bonaventura, p. 112, 190, 345 and 406.

31 The majority of the biblical citations are taken from the King James Bible (Authorised Version); where the English was ambiguous or obscure, the New English Bible translation was used. For a translation in Middle Dutch of the passage from Isaiah 32:9-20, see Bible in duytsche 1477.

32 It is interesting in this connection to point out a comparison with the painting in Genoa, where the same forest scene occurs. Apparently the tower on this building was a kind of dovecote or pigeon house (see the essay by Yvette Bruijnen in this catalogue). In background landscapes by Joachim Patinir and Jerome Bosch, the presence of a dovecote beside a farm dwelling usually intimated that the house was a brothel – a 'house of pleasure' – and perhaps it has a similar meaning in David's painting. On the significance of the dovecote see Bax 1979, p. 295 and Falkenburg 1988, p. 71.

33 Goosen 1990, pp. 119-20; Bieritz 1988, pp. 173-74. Texts from Isaiah were also used in the so-called prophets' drama, also known as Ordo Prophetarum, that was performed in the church around Christmas time; see Young 1921 and Young 1933, pp. 125-71. This dramatic performance, which had developed from a sermon, presented the figures of the prophets 'on stage' proclaiming the birth of Christ by citations from their writings. Isaiah was a prominent figure in this play and also appeared even in abbreviated versions. Various authors have suggested that there is a reference to this prophet's play in the panel showing Christ's Nativity, by Hugo van der Goes (p. 17, fig. 4) in which two bearded figures stand to the right and the left and pull open a curtain, thus revealing the birth of the Christ Child. It has been said that these two figures represent the prophets Isaiah and Habakuk (see note 24) because the presence of the ox and ass beside the manger is based on their texts; see Knipping 1942, p. 63 and Ridderbos 1991, pp. 194-95.

34 Prophecies of Isaiah that were often connected with Christ's Nativity include: Isaiah 7:14-16; 9:1-6; 11:1-16. For prophecies of Isaiah that were connected by late medieval writers with the Passion of Christ and thus influenced the iconography of the Passion, see Marrow 1979.

35 We know from extant contracts that the fifteenth-century painter Dieric Bouts had to follow the instructions of theologians from the university of Louvain for some of his important commissions, see Schöne 1938, p. 240, doc. 55 and p. 243, doc. 70.

36 Harbison 1990, p. 74.

37 Rohlmann 1995.

38 For the iconography of the rest on the flight to Egypt, see Schwartz 1975 and Kofuku 1990.

39 Wertheim Aymès 1957, p. 42; Wertheim Aymès 1961, p. 10 and 80.

40 Friedmann 1980, pp. 146-47, 299; Roth-Bojadzhiev 1985, pp. 37-38.

CATALOGUE

Ariane van Suchtelen

1 GERARD DAVID (c.1450-1523)

Triptych with the Nativity, Donors and Saints Jerome and Leonard, c.1505-1515

Panels transferred onto canvas, 90.2 × 71.1 cm
(centre piece) and 90.2 × 31.4 cm (wings)
The Metropolitan Museum of Art, New York,
The Jules S. Bache Collection, 1949

Outside wings: *Forest Scene, c.1505-1515*
Panel, 30.7 × 89.9 cm (each)
Mauritshuis, The Hague (on loan from the Rijksmuseum, Amsterdam)

TECHNICAL ASPECTS *The measurements of the painted surface of the two panels in the Mauritshuis are the original ones. The barbe can be seen on all sides (the painted surface of each panel measures 88.2 × 28.8 cm). Infrared reflectography of the* Forest Scene *reveals scarcely any underdrawing (The Central Laboratory Amsterdam, 1985). Infrared reflectography of the triptych in New York reveals a very fragmentary underdrawing (M. Ainsworth, The Metropolitan Museum of Art, New York, 1983). This suggests that large portions of the ground and underdrawing were lost when the triptych was transferred onto canvas. The adhesive with which the painting was attached to the new canvas, interferes with the radiographic image. For information on the X-radiographs of the* Forest Scene *and other technical aspects, see the article by Yvette Bruijnen in this catalogue.*

PROVENANCE *Ramon F. Urrutia Collection, Madrid, 1920; art dealers Duveen Brothers, Paris, 1928; J.S. Bache Collection, New York, 1928 (the complete triptych).*

The wings were sawn apart, sometime between 1930 and 1932. The outside wings returned to Duveen Brothers; purchased by the Rijksmuseum, Amsterdam, 1932 (inv.nos. Sk-A-3134/3135), on loan to the Mauritshuis since 1948; inv.no. 843.

The centre piece and the inside wings on loan from J.S. Bache to The Metropolitan Museum of Art, New York since 1943; bequeathed in 1949; inv.no. 49.7.20a-c.

BIBLIOGRAPHY *Mayer 1920, p. 97, ill.; Friedländer 1924-37, VI (1928), p. 143, no. 160, XIV (1937), p. 106, no. 160; cat. Bache 1929, ill.; Heil 1929, p. 4, fig. p. 7; Antwerp 1930, pp. 33-34, no. 95; Burrows 1930, p. 452, fig. opposite p. 449; Cortissoz 1930, p. 258; Mayer 1930, p. 542; Annual Report Rijksmuseum 1932, pp. 8-9, ill.; cat. Amsterdam 1934, pp. 79-80, nos. 767 b & c; Baldass 1936, pp. 94-95; cat. Duveen 1941, no. 181, ill.; Wehle 1943, p. 288; cat. Bache 1944, no. 20, ill.; Burroughs 1945, fig. on cover; The Hague 1945, pp. 38-39, no. 47; Louchheim 1945-46, pp. 58-59, ill.; Nieburg 1946, ill.; Boon 1946, p. 51, pp. 54-56, ill.; Glavimans 1946, pp. 55-56, no. 1, ill.; Wehle/Salinger 1947, pp. 95-96; Van Puyvelde 1947, no. 30, pl. III; Bruges 1949, pp. 15-16, no. 4, ill., pl. VI; London 1949, pp. 11-12, no. 8, pl. III; D'Otrange 1951, pp. 207-09, ill.; Panofsky 1953, I, p. 470, note 1; Allen/Gardner 1954, p. 27; Marlier 1957, pp. 88-89, 124; Larsen 1960, pp. 80-81, 125-26, figs 25a-c; Winkler 1964, p. 152, note 4; Stechow 1966, p. 64, fig. 118; Cuttler 1968, p. 197, fig. 247; Koch 1968, p. 66; Van Puyvelde 1968, p. 211; Tóth-Ubbens 1968, pp. 21-22, ill.; Whinney 1968, pp. 113-14; Von der Osten/Vey 1969, p. 307; Friedländer 1967-76, VIb (1971), p. 100, no. 160, pl. 163-65; Pochat 1973, pp. 245-46; Lane 1975, p. 485, fig. 16; Scillia 1975, pp. 239-40; Leningrad/Moscow 1975, no. 16; Heller 1976, p. 186, no. 91; Van Thiel et al. 1976, p. 189, ill.; Hoetink/Duparc 1977, p. 71, no. 843; Morse 1979, p. 92; Baetjer 1980, I, p. 43, III, fig. p. 347; Châtelet 1980, pp. 174-75, fig. 149; Mundy 1980, p. 38; Lane 1984, p. 53, p. 55, fig. 34; Luijten 1984, p. 384, 421; Snyder 1985, pp. 191-92, figs 187-88; Hoetink 1985, pp. 170-71, ill., p. 356, no. 843; Haverkamp Begemann/Chong 1985, pp. 57-58, p. 66, note 6; Vlieghe 1985, pp. 102-03; Bauman 1986, pp. 28-30, ill.; Hand/Wolff 1986, p. 121, ill.; Genaille 1986, p. 68, p. 70, fig. 5; Broos 1988, pp. 64-65, ill.; Amsterdam/Boston/Philadelphia 1987-88, p. 16; Hänschke 1988, p. 19; Gibson 1989, p. 78; Van Miegroet 1989, pp. 230-34, figs 218-20, p. 300, no. 30, ill.; Haasse 1989, ill.; Cleven 1990, ill.; Ainsworth 1990, p. 652; Bauman et al. 1992, p. 327, no. 176; Devisscher 1992, p. 191; Sluijter-Seijffert et al. 1993, p. 51, no. 843, ill.; Wood 1993, pp. 40-41, fig. 24; Ainsworth 1994a, p. 489; Harbison 1995, pp. 137-38, figs 95-96; Ridderbos 1995, pp. 123-25, fig. 31; Härting 1995, ill.; Baetjer 1995, p. 260. (Compiled by Y. Bruijnen and E. Buijsen.)*

Colourplates on pp. 14-15.

2 HANS MEMLING (c.1440-1494)

Portrait of a man from the Lespinette family, c.1485-1490

Reverse: a coat of arms
Panel, 30.1 × 22.3 cm
Mauritshuis, The Hague

With a great feeling for lifelike detail Hans Memling has portrayed this man in close-up, against a background landscape. The sitter is wearing a mantle trimmed with lynx fur, rings on his fingers and a pendant set with pearls. With his dark curls and the scar on his broad nose he cuts a striking figure. This painting was not produced as an independent portrait, but certainly formed part of a diptych with the Virgin and Child on the left wing. The man in the portrait would have addressed his prayers to them. When closed this devotional diptych would have displayed the man's family arms which are painted on the reverse of the panel.[1] The helmet element of this coat of arms consists of a tournament helmet with six visor bars, a coil of cloth and a falcon with outspread wings and bells attached to its legs. The cover is formed by stylized oak leaves. The escutcheon has been painted over at some point in the past, possibly on the orders of a new owner. However, the original arms have now been reconstructed with certainty as those of the Lespinette family of Franche-Comté, a region which belonged to the Burgundian Hapsburg Empire at the time the work was produced.[2] Which member of this French family was painted by the renowned Bruges portraitist in the late fifteenth century has yet to be established.

The *Virgin and Child* which accompanied this portrait is no longer known. Only two such diptychs by Memling have survived intact. One of these is the *Diptych of Maarten van Nieuwenhove* from 1487 (fig. 1), whose original frames with inscriptions have also been preserved.[3] The inscription identifying the sitter and the date of the Lespinette portrait was probably lost along with the original frame. The (painted) frames in Memling's portraits, which often created the illusion of a window frame, played an important role in the spatial effect of the presentation.

A variation on the devotional diptych with praying patron on the right wing is provided by a rare Memling triptych which comprised three panels of equal dimensions.[4] In this work, whose panels have become separated and dispersed, the Florentine Benedetto Portinari, portrayed on the right wing, prays to the Virgin on the centre panel. Portinari was one of a legion of foreign merchants and bankers who were active in Bruges during this period. The painting on the left wing represents his patron saint Benedict. It cannot be excluded that the Lespinette portrait, in which the praying figure is also turned to the left, originally formed part of a similar triptych. Memling's famous *Portrait of a Man Praying* in the Thyssen-Bornemisza collection in Madrid, with a beautiful still life of flowers on the reverse, presumably once served as the left wing in a triptych of a more usual type.[5] The man, who turns to the right, was originally accompanied by a portrait of his wife on the right wing, both praying to the Virgin on the centre panel. Thus the man occupied the place of honour to the right of the Blessed Mother and Child (left from the viewer's perspective), a position assigned to St Benedict on the Portinari triptych.

The devotional diptych with praying patron on the right wing and Virgin and Child on the left wing first occurs in the œuvre of Memling's probable master, Rogier van der Weyden (c.1400-1464), who worked in Brussels.[6] Such diptychs of modest dimensions were not designed for permanent display on the wall but were kept closed, in a case of velvet, felt or leather. The existence of such cases is known from written sources and a single surviving example: a French diptych with portraits of Roy René and Jeanne Laval from around 1476 which has been preserved with its original red velvet case (fig. 2).[7] The diptych to which the Lespinette portrait must have belonged

1 Hans Memling, Diptych of Maarten van Nieuwenhove. *Panel, 44.7 × 33.5 cm (each). Memling Museum, Bruges.*

was possibly kept in a similar manner. During use it was opened and placed on a surface or hung on a wall, so that the owner was led in his personal prayers to the Virgin and Child by his own praying image.

Hans Memling, who is generally regarded as a somewhat conservative artist, was an innovative portrait painter. Always portrayed three-quarter view, his figures are usually fitted tightly into the painting frame: the hands are often cut off by the edge. Memling was the first northern artist to paint portraits against a landscape, thereby creating a feeling of great space. This indicates that he was probably influenced by the Italian open-air portrait.[8] Also, Rogier van der Weyden's *Triptych of Jean de Braque*, now in the Louvre, would have been a source of inspiration.[9] In this work saints are represented half-length against a panoramic landscape. Although the chronology of Memling's œuvre is sometimes difficult to

establish, owing to a certain evenness in his style, this portrait of a scion of the Lespinette family can be dated to *c.*1485-1490 on the basis of dendrochronological research.[10]

TECHNICAL ASPECTS *The painting, which is in a fine state of preservation, has essentially retained its original dimensions: only a little wood has been planed off along the right edge. The elongated clouds are a later addition, while the escutcheon on the reverse is also a later overpainting.*

Infrared reflectography reveals that the hands are underdrawn in a dry drawing medium (J.R.J. van Asperen de Boer, 1979).[11] In the painting the fingers are positioned some five millimetres to the left.

Dendrochronological analysis of the panel revealed the earliest felling date of 1474, the most likely felling date being 1480 onwards (P. Klein, 1994).[12]

PROVENANCE *Sir Andrew Fontaine Collection, Harfold Hall, Norfolk, before 1850; his sale 7 July 1894, lot no. 46 (as Antonella da Messina); purchased in 1895 by the Vereniging Rembrandt, ownership transferred to the State for display in the Mauritshuis; inv.no. 595.*

LITERATURE *Bredius 1895, pp. 228-29; Martin 1935, pp. 197-98; Friedländer 1967-76, VI (1971), no. 79; Tóth-Ubbens 1968, pp. 37-38; Broos 1987, no. 40 (with extensive literature); Dülberg 1990, no. 11; De Vos 1994, no. 40; Bruges 1994, no. 18.*

1 For other examples of portraits with family coats of arms on the reverse see: Dülberg 1990, nos. 1-126.

2 The original escutcheon beneath this overpainting consists of: above, a band sanguine (extending to about 1 cm beneath the present white band) with three gilded discs or crescents increasing in size above, and below a field azure with a gilded chevron (with thanks to R. Hoppenbrouwers who studied the underlying painting in raking light, through the lacunae in the upper paint layers, and on an x-radiograph). See: Rietstap 1884-87, II, p. 56; Rietstap 1903-26, IV (1912), fig. LIII. For a contour drawing of this escutcheon see: Martin 1935, pp. 197-98. Tóth-Ubbens 1968, pp. 37-38, seems to have confused the original escutcheon with the overpainted one.

3 De Vos 1994, no. 78. The reverse of these panels now shows no traces of painting. The family arms of Van Nieuwenhove are depicted in a stained-glass window behind the Virgin. For the second example see: De Vos, 1994, no. 55.

4 De Vos 1994, no. 79

5 De Vos 1994, no. 72

6 See Hulin de Loo 1923, who was the first to reconstruct three of Rogier van der Weyden's devotional diptychs. On the master-apprenticeship relationship between Van der Weyden and Memling see: Ainsworth 1994b.

7 See Dülberg 1990, pp. 41-43, 88, 89 and no. 174.

8 De Vos 1994, pp. 365-70.

9 Friedländer 1967-76, II (1967), no. 26.

10 Klein 1994.

11 For underdrawing in Memling's work see: Ainsworth 1994b, in particular pp. 84-86 on portraits. See also: Buijsen 1996, pp. 62-67.

12 See Klein 1994, p. 103.

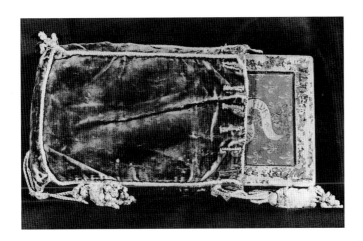

2 Closed diptych with portraits of Roy René and Jeanne Laval, c.1474. In original red velvet case. Panel, 17.7 × 13.4 cm (each). Musée du Louvre, Paris.

3 JAN PROVOOST (c.1464-1529)

Triptych with the Virgin and Child, John the Evangelist and
Mary Magdalene, c.1520-1525

Exterior panels: imitation porphyry
Panel, 44 × 30.5 cm (centre panel) and 49.5 × 15 cm
(wings)
Mauritshuis, The Hague (on loan
from the Rijksmuseum, Amsterdam)

1 Albrecht Dürer, a St Anne and Joachim at the Golden Gate, 1504, b The Betrothal of the Virgin, c The Glorification of the Virgin. Woodcuts, 29.3 × 20.7 cm. Rijksprentenkabinet, Amsterdam.

Quite exceptionally, this triptych by Jan Provoost has survived in its beautifully-painted, original frame. Around the centre panel, which depicts the Virgin and Child, the frame is decorated with motifs derived from woodcuts by Albrecht Dürer (1471-1528). The frames around the wings, which portray John the Evangelist and Mary Magdalene, are marbled. The reverse sides of the wings are painted in imitation of green and red porphyry, with a turquoise marbled frame.

The landscape background on the centre panel, with a charming view of a city to the right, is not continued into the paintings on the wings.[1] Unlike the Virgin on the centre panel, the figures on the side wings are presented full-length, giving rise to a theory that the wings did not initially belong with this centre piece. However, this theory was refuted when the authenticity of the frame was established.[2]

On the centre panel the Virgin is enthroned behind a parapet which extends the frame and resembles a window sill. The Christ Child is seated on this parapet, on a richly worked cushion. A goldfinch is perched on his hand. According to legend, when this little bird pulled a thorn from Christ's forehead, a drop of blood coloured its head. The goldfinch features as an attribute of the Christ Child chiefly in fifteenth-century Italian art, and alludes to Christ's future suffering.[3] In Provoost's painting the function of the goldfinch has been somewhat attenuated, as its head is no longer red. The little bird is attached by a chain to a small majolica vase which is decorated with Christ's monogram. The vase contains red roses and lilies-of-the-valley, symbols of the Virgin's Immaculate Concep-tion and her virginity.[4] The motifs on the frame around the centre panel have been copied almost exactly from three woodcuts by Dürer from a series on the life of the Virgin.

These appeared in book form in 1511 (figs 1 a-c).[5] In the lower centre of the frame, Moses is seated with the old tablets of the law (cp. fig. 1c), between two owls (cp. fig. 1b) which symbolize the synagogue. Together these motifs represent the Old Covenant which came to end when Christ appeared on earth. Old Testament figures feature on the side sections of the frame (cp. fig. 1a). Amongst the curves and curlicues which decorate the top section, small figures seated on unicorns fight opponents on lions (cp. fig. 1b).[6] As a rule the unicorn symbolizes Mary's victorious virginity.

On the left wing John is depicted as a disciple. When represented as an evangelist he is generally grey and bearded, but as the beloved disciple of Jesus, he appears young and clean-shaven.[7] In his hands John holds up a chalice from which a snake is writhing. The source for this attribute is an apocryphal tale disseminated through the *Legenda Aurea*.[8] The story goes that a priest from the temple of Diana in Ephesus tried to test the strength of John's faith by making him drink from a cup of poison which had just caused the death of two condemned men. John made the sign of the cross over the cup and drank up the poison without suffering any harm. As an attribute of John in his role as disciple and apostle, the chalice represents the Christian church while the snake is Satan vanquished.[9] On the right wing Mary Magdalene can be identified from her pot of ointment. She was the repentant sinner who proved her love for Jesus by washing and anointing his feet. Here she is portrayed as a wealthy woman of the world, wearing a costly girdle and headdress. According to a later legend, she spent many years as a hermit in a cave near Sainte-Baume, in France.[10] In the background right of the painting she is depicted a second time, as a long-haired hermit at the entrance to a cave.

In 1494, the same year that his illustrious forebear Hans Memling died, Jan Provoost who originally came from Mons in Hainault, gained burghership of Bruges. Gerard David was also working in Bruges at that time. Provoost's career as a painter flourished in that city and from 1501 he regularly held senior positions in the painters' Guild of St Luke. He probably maintained commercial and artistic contacts with Antwerp as well, where he had been a member of the guild since 1493. When Dürer was travelling through the Low Countries in 1520-21, Provoost accompanied him from Antwerp to Bruges. The renowned German artist also stayed with Provoost, which is further proof of Provoost's status as a leading painter.[11]

Unlike Dürer, Provoost never signed or dated his paintings. His œuvre has been reconstructed on the basis of only two documented works from his later years, a *Virgin Mary as the Queen of Heaven* from 1524, which was destined for the altar dedicated to the prophet Daniel in the St Donatus Church in Bruges, and a *Last Judgement* from 1525, painted for the town hall of Bruges.[12] Although the same hand can be clearly recognized in this triptych of the Virgin and Child, dating of the work remains uncertain. The motifs derived from Dürer may point to a date around or after 1511, the year in which Dürer's series of prints on the life of the Virgin was published in book form. However, some of these sheets had been published several years previously. Another hypothesis is that these derivations were inspired by Provoost's meeting with Dürer, and that this work was painted in the early 1520s.[13]

Given the modest dimensions of Provoost's triptych, it was presumably intended for domestic use. The exemplary love for Christ shown by the saints depicted on the wings would undoubtedly have encouraged the owner's devotion during his or her prayers to the Christ Child, who is emphatically displayed by his Mother. When closed this triptych appears to be a rich object made of marble and porphyry, stones to which eternal value was attributed.[14] The symbolism of such costly materials is entirely appropriate in the context of the religious imagery on the inside of the triptych.

TECHNICAL ASPECTS *Technical research has revealed several changes in composition made by Provoost on the centre panel. Originally, four columns were planned to the left and right of the Virgin, two in the foreground and two in the background. A cloth over the balustrade has also been painted out. The golden ornamentation (the Virgin and Child's haloes, details in the architectural decoration and the cushion) has been partially overpainted with lead tin yellow (presumably before c.1720 when this pigment fell out of use). Probably at the same time the original cloth behind the Virgin was overpainted.*

Infrared reflectography revealed an underdrawing in a black drawing medium (M. Faries and R. Spronk, 1994, 1995). The sketchy drawing style of the centre panel differs from that of the wings, allowing a connection to be established between the various styles of underdrawing within the group of paintings attributed to Provoost.[15]

Although it was suspected that the painted decoration on the frame of the centre panel was a later addition, this could not be confirmed by study of paint samples. The original hanging ring has been preserved. Since its restoration in 1996, the triptych has regained its rich, vivid colouring.

PROVENANCE *C. Hoogendijk Collection, Amsterdam; since 1907 on loan to the Rijksmuseum; in 1912 presented to the Rijksmuseum (inv.no. Sk-A-2570); since 1924 on loan to the Mauritshuis; inv.no. 783.*

LITERATURE *Jaarverslag Rijksmuseum (Annual Report) 1912, p. 16; Winkler 1924, p. 144; Friedländer 1967-76, ixb (1973), no. 122; Tóth-Ubbens 1968, pp. 46-47; Van Thiel et al. 1976, p. 457; Brussels 1977, no. 304; Roberts 1987, pp. 12-16; Henkels 1993, p. 236, 240; Spronk 1993, 1, pp. 58-59, 60, 62-63, 195; Pottasch 1994.*

1 A striking feature in this work is the bare tree in front of the townscape. The meaning of this motif is not clear (possibly a symbol for death, compare *Lexikon Christlicher Kunst*, Freiburg 1980, p. 54). There is also a bare tree in the background of Provoost's *The Virgin as Queen of Heaven;* Friedländer 1967-76, ixb (1973), no. 177. For a later example of this motif see: Broos 1987, p. 354.

2 See Pottasch 1994.

3 See Friedmann 1946.

4 Both symbols originally derive from the Song of Solomon (2:1). See Levi d'Ancona 1977, pp. 221, 330-55.

5 For this series see: Panofsky 1945, p. 96 ff. Hollstein (German), vii, pp. 154-64, nos. 189-208, in particular nos. 191, 194 and 207.

6 In Dürer's work the small figures on the lions are female.

7 Hall 1979, pp. 174-75. Goosen (1992, pp. 127-35) points out the different ways of representing St John in eastern and western art.

8 James of Voragine, *Legenda Aurea, c.*1280. This is a collection of saints' lives which are described in the order of the liturgical calendar. Between 1470 and 1500 alone, more than a hundred editions of this work were published in translation as well as in the original Latin. In 1505 and 1516 Dutch translations were published in Antwerp.

9 See the literature mentioned in note 7.

10 In western tradition three biblical Marys have been combined in one person. See: Hall 1979, pp. 202-04.

11 See: Brussels 1977, pp. 142-43.

12 Friedländer 1967-76, ixb (1973), resp. nos. 177 and 156. For identification of the former painting see: Spronk 1993, 1, p. 32, note 130.

13 See: Tóth-Ubbens 1968, p. 57.

14 For the use of imitation marble and its significance see: Dülberg 1990, pp. 116-27.

15 See: Spronk 1993, Pottasch 1994.

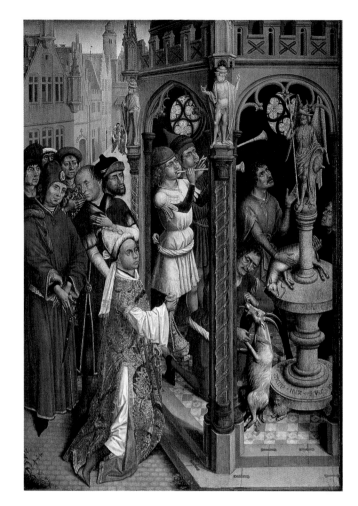 

4 UNKNOWN MASTER FROM BRUSSELS

a *Augustine Sacrificing to an Idol of the Manichaeans?*, *c.*1480

Panel, 97.3 × 68.3 cm
Mauritshuis, The Hague (on loan
from the Rijksmuseum, Amsterdam)

b *Augustine Healing a Sick Man and Baptizing Heathens?*, *c.*1480

Panel, 98.3 × 67 cm
National Gallery of Ireland, Dublin

1 *Master of St Gudule,*
The Preaching of
St Augustine?, *c.1480.*
Panel, 97.7 × 68.7 cm.
Musée du Louvre, Paris.

2 Rogier van der Weyden,
The Lamentation of Christ,
c.1450. Panel, 80.6 × 130.1 cm.
Mauritshuis, The Hague.

These panels from Dublin and The Hague originally formed part of the same ensemble, possibly an altarpiece dedicated to St Augustine.[1] They were painted by one of the anonymous Brussels masters who was still working in the style of Rogier van der Weyden (*c.*1400-1464) in the late fifteenth century (cp. fig. 2). These masters often collaborated closely when commissioned to produce large altarpieces.

A panel in the Louvre of identical size and related composition, *The Preaching of St Augustine?*, probably belonged to the same work (fig. 1). This painting is by another artist, the Master of St Gudule, who has derived his provisional name from the Brussels church with double towers which appears in the background of *The Preaching*.[2] The painting in the Louvre offers a clue to the dating of this ensemble, as the northern tower of St Gudule (today St Michael's Cathedral) is depicted in a half-finished state. Construction of this tower was only completed around 1480-85, from which it may be inferred that the panel in the Louvre was probably produced before this period.[3]

In the past the painting in The Hague was erroneously identified as Solomon's idolatry, while the Dublin panel was believed to show scenes from the life of St Nicholas of Bari.[4] When considered together with the work from the Louvre, the panels were also interpreted as scenes from the life of the holy bishop Géry of Cambrai.[5] Although the latter identification also appears to be incorrect, it does make allowance for the associated subject matter on all three panels which feature the same figure. This is a man in a red robe with a blue stole and purple hat, a costume which marks him as a scholar. Identification of this scholar as St Augustine seems the most probable hypothesis.[6]

Augustine (354-430) was consecrated as bishop of Hippo in 394. Thanks to his many important theological writings, he is renowned as one of the four Fathers of the Church. In his youth he had supported the heretical teachings of the Manichaeans: on the Mauritshuis panel, the young man clad in fanciful liturgical robes who is incensing a heathen sacrifice possibly represents Augustine as a young heretic.[7] He appears again in the left background, this time in the garments of a scholar. In the Dublin painting Augustine appears to be healing a sick man and is baptizing heathens. The two figures to the left in oriental costume may represent the heretics whom Augustine converted to Christianity. The panel in the Louvre, where the protagonist is again represented a second time in the left background, may portray Augustine as a teacher and preacher. If identification of the main figure as Augustine is correct, these panels present fairly unusual episodes from his life, particularly as in other works he is generally depicted in bishop's robes. Nevertheless, these scenes might have been easier to recognize in the context of a large ensemble. In a triptych showing scenes from the life of Augustine, whose middle panel is in New York (fig. 3), the saint's consecration as a bishop occupies centre stage.[8] To the right of this scene Augustine is depicted debating with scholars. Here, he wears the same costume, typical of scholars, as in the three panels under consideration.

The paintings in The Hague and Dublin were attributed by Max Friedländer to the Master of the St Barbara Legend, a Brussels painter whom the German art historian named after two panels showing scenes from the life of St Barbara.[9] The paintings which Friedländer attributed to this master are characterized by compositions with foreground figures in fanciful open buildings, women with high foreheads and men with dishevelled beards. However, not all the paintings in the group assembled by Friedländer are still considered to be by the same artist. For example, in the St Barbara panels just mentioned, the hands of two different masters have now been detected.[10]

Although the paintings here displayed do bear stylistic affinities with the Friedländer group, they were probably produced by another master. Characteristic of his style are the powerful brushstrokes employed in the rendering of facial highlights – with loose locks of hair on the forehead – without any attempt to blend these strokes. The figures are of another type than those in the Barbara panels, who are thinner with angular limbs. The paintings on display belong to a group which has now been dissociated from the œuvre of the Master of the St Barbara Legend. This group is centred around a triptych with scenes showing St Crispin and St Crispinian.[11] The plant motifs in the foreground, which also appear in the Dublin panel, are a trademark of this painter's workshop.[12]

3 Master of St Augustine, Centre
Panel of a Triptych with Scenes
from the Life of Augustine,
*c.1490-1500. Panel, 130 × 153 cm.
The Metropolitan Museum of Art,
New York, The Cloisters
Collection, 1961.*

TECHNICAL ASPECTS *4a The panel has retained its original dimensions. Infrared reflectography has revealed an underdrawing in brush (C. Pottasch, 1996). The praying figure at the far right is a later addition by the painter. Originally a fruit lay at the feet of the figure to the left, but was later painted out.*

The reverse of the panel shows traces of a ground layer, possibly remnants of a protective paint layer.

4b The panel has lost its unpainted left and right edges. The paint surface has been damaged in places. Some underdrawing in brush is visible to the naked eye. Unlike the panel in the Mauritshuis, the reverse shows no traces of a ground layer.

PROVENANCE *4a Possibly W.A. Kien van Citters Collection, Middelburg, 1787 (as Albrecht Dürer); C. Lambrechtsen van Ritthem Collection; bequest to the Middelburg Drawing Academy, 1823; auction Amsterdam (F. Muller), 9 December 1902, no. 37; Rijksmuseum, Amsterdam (inv.no. Sk-A-2057); on loan to the Mauritshuis since 1948; inv.no. 844. 4b Auction Bristol (Christie's), 2 October 1862, no. 125; inv.no. 360.*

LITERATURE *Friedländer 1924-25, pp. 22, 25; Brussels 1935, nos. 49 and 50; Paris 1935, no. 53 (4a); Van de Castyne 1935, Van de Castyne 1936; De Tervarent 1936; Lefèvre/Praem 1936; Brussels 1953, no. 51 (4a); Tóth-Ubbens 1968, pp. 31-32 (4a); Friedländer 1967-76, IV (1969), nos. 66 and 67; Reynaud/Foucart 1970, pp. 68-69; Van Thiel et al. 1976, p. 634 (4a); Vogelaar 1987, pp. 49-53 (4b); Périer-d'Ieteren 1989-91, p. 171, note 22; Périer-d'Ieteren 1994, p. 61, fig. 8b (4a).*

1 It is also possible that these panels belonged to a series of separate paintings showing scenes from the life of the saint (see also Van de Castyne 1935, p. 319). Compare, for example, a series from the same period on St Romolt from Malines Cathedral (Friedländer 1967-76, IV (1969), no. 106, Add. 164 [as Colijn de Coter]; Vogelaar 1987, pp. 53-62). These panels are accompanied by explanatory texts.

2 Friedländer 1924-25, p. 25; Friedländer 1967-76, IV (1969), no. 70.

3 Michel 1953, p. 186

4 For interpretation of the Mauritshuis painting as Solomon's idolatry see: Jaarverslag Rijksmuseum (Annual Report) 1903, p. 13. However, Solomon committed his idolatry as an older man, and the painting also lacks the concubine who seduced him into worshipping images (cp. cat. 7). For the Dublin panel as scenes from the life of St Nicholas of Bari compare: Vogelaar 1987, p. 51.

5 See: De Tervarent 1936, who based this identification on a fourth panel (Musée de Cluny, Paris: Friedländer 1967-76, IV (1969), supp. 116). However, this work belongs in a series of scenes showing the works of charity (see Friedländer 1939, p. 24), which removes the

basis for De Tervarent's identification. Like St Nicholas of Bari, Géry was always portrayed as a bishop.

6 Van de Castyne 1935, Van de Castyne 1936. For the iconography of Augustine see: Courcelle 1965-72, in which these paintings are not, however, discussed.

7 The painting from The Hague bears a remarkable resemblance to a miniature from the *Chroniques de Hainaut* (1448-1449: *The High Priest of the Belgae Consults the Goddess Diana*, Royal Library, Brussels, MS 9242, fol. 175 verso), an illustrated translation of Jacques de Guise's work which was produced for Philip the Good of Burgundy (see Cockshaw 1979). Not only is the composition close, many details are also similar. On the basis of this similarity, Tóth-Ubbens (1968, p. 31) postulates that the Mauritshuis painting represents a historical event, possibly *The High Priest of the Belgae Sacrificing to Mercury?*.

8 Friedländer 1967-76, VIb (1971), supp. 244; Vogelaar 1987, pp. 46-49.

9 Friedländer 1924-25; Friedländer 1967-76, IV (1969), no. 57.

10 See Guislain-Witterman 1978-79.

11 Reynaud/Foucart 1970, pp. 68-70. See: Friedländer 1967-76, IV (1969), Add. 163; Białostocki 1966, pp. 9-13; Hoff/Davies 1971, pp. 14-16, 21; Nikulin 1987, pp. 43-45. Périer-d'Ieteren (1989-91, 1994), once again attributes the altarpiece with St Crispin and St Crispinian, amongst other works, to the Master of the St Barbara Legend. However, she excludes the paintings here displayed, together with several other paintings (Périer-d'Ieteren 1989-91, p. 171, note 22). In a later publication she appears to reconsider her decision and attributes a detail from the Mauritshuis painting to the Master of the St Barbara Legend (Périer-d'Ieteren 1994, fig. 8b). Vogelaar (1987, pp. 49-50) devised the provisional name 'Master of Saints Crispin and Crispinian' for the painter of the Dublin panel.

12 Białostocki (1966, p. 13) presumes a *Musterbuch* was used for the plant motifs.

5 MASTER OF FRANKFURT (ACTIVE *c*.1490-1520)

a *St Catherine*, *c*.1510-1520

b *St Barbara*, *c*.1510-1520

Panel, 158.7 × 70.8 cm (each)
Mauritshuis, The Hague

1 Master of Frankfurt, Holy Family and Music-Making Angels. *Panel, 156.2 × 155.9 cm. Walker Art Gallery, Liverpool.*

The original centre panel of this triptych by the Master of Frankfurt, *The Holy Family with Music-Making Angels* is currently to be found in the Walker Art Gallery in Liverpool (fig. 1). It has been separated from the side wings portraying the saints Catherine and Barbara which are part of the Mauritshuis collection. The landscape originally connected the Holy Family, the angels and the saints in a single, continuous scene.[1] Many kinds of plants and flowers are depicted in the foreground with a strong sense of detail.

In the late Middle Ages the early Christian virgin saints Catherine and Barbara enjoyed great popularity, in the wake of the energetic cult of the Virgin Mary.[2] Catherine was a king's daughter from Alexandria who managed to convert fifty heathen philosophers to Christianity. Enraged by her steadfast godliness, emperor Maxentius had her tortured on a spiked wheel. An angel destroyed this instrument of torture – an event which seems be depicted in the painting background left. When Catharine was eventually beheaded, milk instead of blood flowed from her neck, as a sign of her virginity. Catherine's attributes are the broken wheel, which lies beneath her feet, and the sword. An important episode in her history is her mystical betrothal with Christ, who slipped a ring on her finger in a dream. On account of her important position as the Virgin Mary's 'daughter-in-law', she was considered the most important intercessor for the faithful to Christ after Mary. So she is always represented in the place of honour, at Mary's right side.

The relics of St Barbara were kept in the cloisters of St Bavo Cathedral, Ghent, from 985. This certainly contributed to her great popularity in the Southern Netherlands. Barbara was the daughter of a rich heathen from Asia Minor who kept her locked in a tower. She had three windows built in the tower as a symbol of the Holy Trinity. Like Catherine, she remained steadfast in her Christian faith. When she refused to marry a heathen, her enraged father responded by having her tortured and eventually beheaded. Her most important attribute is the tower with three windows. The ostrich feather which she is holding in this painting was presented to her by Christ in a vision.[3] The iris in the foreground left generally serves as a symbol of the Virgin Mary, but sometimes features in paintings of St Barbara.[4] As the patron saint of sanctified death – which means that the last sacraments have been administered prior to death – she was as important a saint as Catherine.

On the centre panel of this now dismantled triptych, the Virgin Mary is represented as *Maria lactans*, a mother breastfeeding her child.[5] She is in the company of Joseph and four angels playing musical instruments, who are curiously left-handed. She is offering a pear to the Christ Child, a symbol of Christ's love, while the Child's gaze draws the viewer into this intimate moment.[6] Joseph is seated on a stone bench behind the Virgin's throne, holding a rosary and a book in his hands. His characterization as a scholarly and pious man is connected with the growing reverence for his person which developed from the late fifteenth century onwards.[7] The chained monkey holding a pomegranate foreground right refers to the forbidden fruit of the Fall, which was negated by the coming of Christ. It may also represent the sinner in chains.[8] The book on the ground foreground left refers to the (biblical) Word that is here become flesh. The landscape in which the Holy Family and both saints are represented echoes the *hortus conclusus,* the enclosed garden in which Mary was often found in the company of angel musicians or virgin saints.[9] Like the *hortus conclusus,* the white lily foreground left is a familiar symbol of Mary's virginity, and is also derived from the Song of Solomon.[10]

We do not know where this altarpiece – whose iconography was fairly common – originally stood. The presence of both St Catherine and St Barbara makes one suspect that this work may have belonged to one of the many convents or beguinages which were founded during the fifteenth century, a period when the religious life proved extremely attractive, particularly to women. St Barbara and St Catherine often served as the patron saints of such institutions, their chastity and renunciation of the world providing models for devout women.

The painter of this triptych has been misleadingly designated the Master of Frankfurt. However, it was in Antwerp, rather than Germany, that he directed a well-equipped painter's workshop, which was active from around 1490 to at least the second decade of the sixteenth century.[11] Standardization of production was a characteristic feature of this studio in which several assistants worked: identical motifs (such as the brocade patterns in clothing), figures and compositional elements were employed in varying combinations.[12] Drawn patterns, prototypes of compositions and individual motifs were presumably used in the workshop,[13] making it sometimes difficult to detect the master's hand in the products from his workshop.

Virtually the same composition of the piece here discussed has been used in a triptych attributed to Jan Gossaert (*c.*1478-1532), now in Lisbon (fig. 2).[14] This triptych should possibly be dated to the period before Gossaert's trip to Italy in 1508. On the centre panel is the composition with the Holy Family and angel musicians (expanded with two angels in the foreground). Joseph is seated to the left, rather than the right, of the Virgin

2 *Jan Gossaert (attributed to)*,
Triptych with the Holy Family,
St Catherine and St Barbara.
*Panel, 43 × 31 cm (centre panel)
and 43 × 11 cm (wings). Museu de
Art Antiga, Lisbon.*

Mary, and the angels playing their instruments are right-handed. This work is often considered to be the model which the Master of Frankfurt used for his triptych from *c.*1510-1520.[15] A third version of the centre panel by an unknown painter shares a striking detail in common with the Master of Frankfurt's mirror image painting in Liverpool: the leg of the angel playing the recorder is bare while Gossaert's is covered in drapery.[16] This detail is one reason why it is improbable that the Master of Frankfurt based his work on the Lisbon triptych. It is more likely that both triptychs were derived from a common model, as was the third version of the centre panel mentioned above. Gossaert would have simply varied the leg of his angel. In any case there is free improvisation in all versions of the composition. Later variations by followers of the Master of Frankfurt indicate that the common model probably came from his own workshop.[17] The mirror-image composition of the Liverpool painting might be explained by the use of pricked cartoons; it may also have been inspired by a simple need to vary a well-known composition.[18]

Two comparable side wings with representations of St Catherine and St Barbara by a follower of the Master of Frankfurt (Museo Cerralbo, Madrid) have been paint-

3-4 Master of Frankfurt
(follower), St Catherine. Reverse:
The Angel Gabriel. Panel,
91.4 × 52 cm. Waddesdon Manor,
Bucks (The National Trust).

ed on the reverse with the Annunciation. A fragment of a version of the St Catherine wing bears the angel Gabriel on its reverse (figs 3 and 4).[19] This reinforces the suspicion that when closed, the altarpiece under consideration also displayed a painting of the Annunciation.[20]

TECHNICAL ASPECTS *A striking detail in common with the centre panel in Liverpool are the fingerprints in the paint which were used as a means to modify the shadows of the tassels on the clothing.[21]*
Infrared reflectography revealed an underdrawing in brush (J.R.J. van Asperen de Boer with A. ter Brugge and J. Rodenburg, 1996).[22] Infrared reflectography of the centre panel in Liverpool revealed a stylistically similar *underdrawing in brush (D. Crombie and C. Stainer-Hutchins, 1996). In 1988 the Mauritshuis panels were restored.*

PROVENANCE *Collection of George Grenville, first marquis of Buckingham, before 1783-1813; thence by inheritance until c.1900 (as Albrecht Dürer); W. von Pannwitz Collection, Berlin, c.1914; C. von Pannwitz, Bennebroek, to 1940; Stichting Nederlands Kunstbezit, 1946; on loan to the Mauritshuis since 1948, ownership transferred in 1960; inv.nos. 854-855.*

LITERATURE *Friedländer 1915, p. 88; Friedländer 1917, pp. 144-45, 149, no. 35; Compton 1958-59, pp. 5, 7-10, 16, note 1-2; Friedländer 1967-76, VII (1971), no. 137; Tóth-Ubbens 1968, pp. 34-35; Goddard 1984, nos. 44 and 45; Goddard 1985, pp. 411-13, 417, note 11-2; Broos 1993, no. 42 (with extensive bibliography).*

1 Reconstruction by Compton 1958-59. Unfortunately, given its fragile condition, the centre panel could not be loaned. Goddard (1985, p. 411) sees the centre panel as a workshop product, while he attributes the figures on the side wings to the Master himself. Assessment of the centre panel, however, seems to be influenced by the extremely discoloured varnish. The triptych must have already been dismantled when the side wings joined the marquis of Buckingham's collection in the eighteenth century.

2 For the cult of virgin saints and the saints Catherine and Barbara see: Muller 1985. For both saints see: Hall 1979, pp. 58-59, 40-41.

3 See: Muller 1985, p. 97. This is not an iconographical anomaly or innovation (Gibson 1987, p. 85; Broos 1993, p. 345), but a very common attribute of St Barbara. For this motif by the Master of Frankfurt compare: Friedländer 1967-76, VII (1971), nos. 130, 130a, 130d, 131, 134, 136, 136a, 152.

4 See: Behling 1967, p. 38.

5 For the iconography of the Virgin Mary breastfeeding the Infant Christ see: Meiss 1936, p. 453 ff.

6 See: Levi d'Ancona 1977, pp. 296-97.

7 For example see: Gibson 1987, p. 88, note 30.

8 Janson 1952, esp. pp. 107-44, 145-62.

9 For examples by Memling compare: De Vos 1994, nos. 87 and 62.

10 Compare cat. 8.

11 Weiszäcker (1897) gave this unknown master his provisional name which is based on his principal work, an altarpiece representing the Holy Kindred that the master painted around 1505 for the Dominican Church of Frankfurt. See e.g. Friedländer 1917, Goddard 1983 and Goddard 1984. The Master of Frankfurt's year of birth, c.1460, can be deduced from an inscription on his self-portrait (Friedländer 1967-76, VII (1971), no. 163).

12 For the use of brocade patterns see: Goddard 1985.

13 The will, dated 1489, of the Brussels artist Vrancke van der Stockt, provides evidence that painters kept patterns in stock. In addition to his uncompleted works this also leaves 'alle bewerpen ... het sy patroonen oft anders dat op papier gemaakt es' (all designs...be it patterns or otherwise made on paper) to his painter sons (see: Campbell 1976, p. 195).

14 For this triptych see: Rotterdam 1965, no. 1. The attribution is based on two drawings by Gossaert (see Gibson 1987, figs 5 and 6). Gibson rejects the Gossaert attribution (1987, pp. 79-80) and dates it c.1510-1515; those of his opinion include Broos 1993, pp. 351-52. P. van den Brink upholds the traditional Gossaert attribution (oral communication, 1996).

15 See also: Friedländer 1971, p. 149.

16 Compton 1958-59, fig. 4; Gibson 1987, fig. 11: previously on loan to the Rijksmuseum, Amsterdam. This detail was noticed by Gibson 1987, p. 86.

17 Compton 1958-59, p. 8, lists variations by followers on the Master of Frankfurt's triptych which he has reconstructed. The centre panel of Compton's no. 1 (Goddard 1984, no. 47), however, is a variation on Goddard 1984, nos. 33, 34 and 37. Goddard 1984, no. 46 (figs 3 and 4) can be added to Compton's list.
   Several depictions of the Virgin Mary and Child from the studio of Joos van Cleve (Compton 1958-59, nos. 8 and 9, Friedländer 1967-76, IXa (1972), no. 60, 60a, VII, 1971, no. 149) are based, in my opinion, on the painting in Liverpool (rather than vice-versa, as is contended by Gibson 1987, p. 87, Broos 1993, p. 354 and Sander 1993, p. 209, note 17); my grounds for this conviction include the similar direction and the absence of the Child's left leg.

18 The underdrawing on the centre panel includes no indications which could confirm this. For the use of such pricked cartoons see: Dunkerton et al. 1991, in particular pp. 169-70. See also: Ainsworth 1989, pp. 10-11.

19 Compton 1958-59, no. 5 and Goddard 1984, no. 46 respectively. The Gabriel figure derives from a standard version of the Annunciation from the workshop of the Master of Frankfurt: Friedländer 1967-76, VII (1971), nos. 125 and 126.

20 The panels in the Mauritshuis were planed down to accommodate the cradles; this would have removed any painting on the reverse.

21 For a technical description see: Broos 1993, p. 349.

22 Compare the underdrawing of the 'Humbracht triptych' by the Master of Frankfurt (Sander 1993, pp. 368-92), which reveals stylistic differences.

6   UNKNOWN MASTER FROM ANTWERP OR ZEELAND

a   *Meeting of Abraham and Melchizedek, c.1500-1520*

Reverse: *The Synagogue*

b   *Gathering the manna, c.1500-1520*

Reverse: *Ecclesia (The Church)*

Panel, 102 × 71.2 cm (each)

Mauritshuis, The Hague (on loan from the Rijksmuseum, Amsterdam)

These two panels, which are painted on both sides, come from the Gasthuis (Hospital) in Goes, in Zeeland, formerly the Convent of St Agnes. Undoubtedly they originally served as the wings of an altar piece. The central panel of this triptych, painted by an unknown master from the beginning of the sixteenth century, has unfortunately been lost.

The patriarch Abraham is depicted on the left panel. He has removed his helmet and steel gloves as a mark of respect and is kneeling before Melchizedek, the king and high priest, at the gates of Salem. Melchizedek is giving Abraham bread and wine, and blessing him. In the background are some of Melchizedek's retinue and Abraham's forces, with whom he has just returned in triumph (Genesis 14:18-24). The offering of bread and wine is traditionally regarded as a prefiguration of the Eucharist, showing the high priest Melchizedek as a predecessor of Christ.[1] His priestly role is further emphasized by the small statue in the portal behind him: a figure crowned by a papal tiara, holding a round loaf in one hand and raising the other hand in blessing.

On the right panel there is also a scene which anticipates the Eucharist. The Israelites, who feared they would starve in the desert during their journey to the Promised Land, are gathering the manna which God rains down upon them (Exodus 16:11-36; Numbers 11:7-9). They are collecting it in baskets and their clothing, while a woman in the centre is holding up a salver which resembles a paten. To the left their leader Moses is pointing out the divine miracle in the form of 'wafers' falling from heaven. This rain of manna is interpreted as a precursor of the Eucharist in the Gospel of St John: 'For the bread of God is he which cometh down from heaven, and giveth life unto the world' (John 6:33).[2]

When the triptych was closed, the grisailles on the reverse of the wings could be seen. These portray personifications of the Synagogue and Ecclesia, the Church, symbolizing the Old Covenant of the Jews and the New Covenant of Christ's Church. The Synagogue is depicted as a blindfolded woman with a broken staff and the tablets of the law bearing the first two commandments, to which is apparently blind.[3] On the right panel the personification of the Christian Church, Ecclesia, holds a chalice above which hovers a wafer. She wears the habit of a Poor Clare, an allusion to St Clare who allegedly managed to ward off a Saracen attack by holding up a wafer.[4] The wafer and chalice in this picture have been wantonly scratched at some point in the past, as have the faces of Melchizedek and Moses.

As the wings depict Old Testament events which may be interpreted as prefigurations of the Eucharist, it might be conjectured that the missing central panel of this triptych represented the Last Supper, when Christ's blessing of bread and wine established the basis for this sacrament in the disciples' first holy communion. The personifications of Ecclesia and Synagogue on the exterior panels thus form a suitable prelude for the message on the interior panels of the original altarpiece: that redemption can be achieved through the holy sacrament of the Church.[5]

A well-known early example of a sacramental altarpiece is the triptych which Dieric Bouts painted in 1464 for the Corpus Christi Brotherhood of St Peter's Church in Louvain (fig. 1).[6] The commission was precisely specified in a contract, and two theologians were engaged to assist the painter. This particular triptych was probably commissioned to mark the two hundredth anniversary of the introduction of the major church feast of Corpus Christi, which was devoted to the cult of the holy sacrament.

1 Dieric Bouts, Sacramental altarpiece, *1464. Panel, 180 × 151 cm
(centre panel) and 88.5 × 71.5 cm
(four side panels). St Peter's
Church, Louvain.*

2 *Master of the Groote Adoration,*
Sacramental altarpiece. *Panel,*
119.5 × 86 cm (centre panel) and
119.5 × 43 cm (wings).
The Metropolitan Museum of Art,
New York, Gift of J. Pierpont
Morgan, 1917.

On the panels to either side of *The Last Supper*, Bouts also painted *The Meeting of Abraham and Melchizedek* and *The Gathering of Manna*, together with representations of *The Jewish Passover* and *Elijah's Dream*, which are further Old Testament prefigurations of the Eucharist.

Given the provenance of the two panels here discussed, the Convent of St Agnes in Goes, it is conceivable that the unknown painter came from Zeeland. All that we know for certain is that the artist was influenced by the Antwerp school of painting. Comparison with a triptych by the Master of the Groote Adoration, an unidentified Antwerp painter from the early sixteenth century, comprising *The Last Supper, The Meeting of Abraham and Melchizedek* and *The Gathering of Manna* (fig. 2), confirms that the panels in the Mauritshuis derive from the same (Antwerp) models: the composition of the left panel, with Abraham kneeling before Melchizedek who is represented to the right in front of the city gates, and the woman raising her salver on the right panel, show a remarkable similarity.[7]

When the panels of the Goes triptych became separated is not known. Perhaps it was during the Iconoclastic Fury which raged through Goes in 1578, that the faces of Melchizedek and Moses, and particularly the Host and chalice in the grisaille of the Church, were attacked with a sharp implement by a fanatical reformer.

TECHNICAL ASPECTS The paint surface has especially suffered on the back of the panels (the most vulnerable side). Also, on the front are large losses in the red areas. Possibly the preparation of the ground is responsible for the small scale pitting which is seen overall, in all four paintings. The brocade pattern on Melchizedek's and Moses' clothing is identical.

Infrared reflectography has revealed a sketchy underdrawing in a dry material (J.R.J. van Asperen de Boer with M. Sarnowiec, 1994). The paintings were restored in 1996.

PROVENANCE Gasthuis, Goes (formerly the Convent of St Agnes); purchased by the National Museum for History and Art, 1876, Rijksmuseum, (inv.nos. Sk-A-866/867); on loan to the Mauritshuis since 1960; inv.nos. 944-945.

LITERATURE Tóth-Ubbens 1968, pp. 42-43; Van Thiel et al. 1976, p. 647; Utrecht 1988, no. 6.

1 See also: Hebrews 5:6, 10; 6:20; 7:1, 10, 11, 15, 17, 21; Psalms 110:4; Christ as priest 'for ever after the order of Melchizedek'.

2 See also: John 6:30-35; Hebrews 9:4; Revelation 2:17. This subject can also be regarded as a prefiguration of Christ's feeding of the five thousand: Hall 1979, p. 215.

3 On the law tablets: 'DILIGE/DOMINV[M]/DEUM/TUUM/EX TOTO/CORDE/TUO' and 'ET PROX/IMUM/TUUM/SICUT/TE IP/SUM' ('Thou shalt love the Lord thy God with all thy heart ... [and] thy neighbour as thyself', Matthew 22:37, 39).

4 Vloberg 1946, II, pp. 262-65.

5 On the centre panel of a presumably southern Netherlandish sacramental altarpiece from 1515, in the Musée Rolin in Autun (see Tóth-Ubbens 1968, p. 43) both Ecclesia and Synagogue are depicted as sculptured elements of the architecture above Christ's head in *The Last Supper*. See: Vloberg 1946, I, p. 40, 101. This further reinforces the supposition that the missing centre panel also represented the Last Supper.

6 See: Neilsen Blum 1969, pp. 59-70. Several other commissioned sacramental altarpieces are known, such as Pieter Pourbus's 1559 painting for the Corpus Christi Brotherhood of St Saviour's Church in Bruges (see: Bruges 1984, no. 6) and Jan de Molder's 1513 work for the Abbey of Averbode (see Jacobs 1994, p. 84 ff.).

7 Compare also panels from two Antwerp retables with sculptured figure groups: Antwerp 1993, no. 9; Friedländer 1967-76, XI (1974), pl. 31.

7 MASTER OF THE SOLOMON TRIPTYCH

Triptych with the Story of Solomon, c.1521

Exterior panels: angels supporting escutcheons
with coats of arms
Panel, 107.5 × 77 cm (centre panel) and 107.5 × 32.5 cm
(wings)
Mauritshuis, The Hague

The idolatry of Solomon is the central theme of this triptych which was painted around 1521 by an anonymous master. When the triptych is closed, the reverse of the wings can be seen, with angels supporting escutcheons with coats of arms against a marbled background. These are the arms of its first owners, Willem Simonz, lord of Stavenisse and Comstrijen (1498-1557) and Adriana van Duyveland (1506-1545). The triptych remained in the possession of the same Zeeland family until it was bequeathed to the State of the Netherlands in 1876, for display in the Mauritshuis.[1]

Despite his proverbial wisdom, Solomon, the Old Testament king of Israel, kept many concubines, who managed to seduce him into raising an altar for their idols (1 Kings 11). The centre panel shows Solomon worshipping at this altar. The episode of Solomon's idolatry is regarded as an example of Women's Tricks: it is one of a number of love stories from antiquity or the Old Testament, in which an otherwise pious or wise man brings ridicule or ruin upon himself as a result of a feminine wiles. Solomon kneels before the idol, watched by a crowd of bystanders and guided by a woman who represents all his concubines. The idol stands on a rickety pedestal of love deities and a sphere. The picture is based on a woodcut showing Solomon's idolatry by Lucas van Leyden (1494?-1533) from a series of works depicting Old Testament stories of women's tricks (fig. 1).[2] In the woodcut the idol is Moloch with his bull's horns, the 'abomination of the Ammonites', to whom children were sacrificed as burnt offerings. Although the anonymous master has borrowed Van Leyden's brazier, his idol is female. This is also the case in some old prints of this subject, adding weight to the theme of women's tricks.[3] The painting on the centre panel of this triptych also deviates from the biblical text in another respect: the altar has not been raised in the open air but within a richly-decorated structure which evokes descriptions of Solomon's temple in Jerusalem.[4]

The left panel shows Solomon's wisdom which could not, however, save him from ruin, and the right panel depicts him facing divine retribution. On the left panel the Queen of Sheba kneels before Solomon and presents him with gifts. She has come to Jerusalem with a large retinue to test his wisdom with complicated riddles (1 Kings 10). In the background, to the left, the camels of her cortege can be discerned. Impressed by Solomon's erudition and the splendour of his court, she praises God who has placed Solomon on the throne. The right panel shows the consequences of Solomon's idolatry, a subject which is possibly depicted for the first time in this work. Solomon kneels before a manifestation of God, in the guise of His Son. The rift in Solomon's kingdom, the penalty which God imposes for Solomon's faithlessness, is represented by the ruptured earth in the background which separates Solomon from his troops. The scene on the right panel also derives from a print by Lucas van Leyden, this time a 1514 engraving showing Solomon's idolatry (fig. 2).[5] Evidence that the anonymous master used Van Leyden's print as a model is strengthened by Solomon's identical headgear in both works. The feathered concoction on the concubine's head in the print is also echoed on the right panel of the triptych in the broad fan of feathers on the helmet of one of Solomon's companions.

Stories on the theme of women's tricks were regarded as cautionary tales, warning of the pernicious influence which a woman could exercise when she was not a man's lawfully-wedded wife. From the beginning of the

1 *Lucas van Leyden,* The Idolatry of
Solomon, *c.1517. Woodcut, 24.2 × 17.1
cm. Rijksprentenkabinet, Amsterdam.*

2 *Lucas van Leyden,* The Idolatry of
Solomon, *1514. Engraving, 16.9 × 12.8
cm. Rijksprentenkabinet, Amsterdam.*

73

3 *Master of the Solomon Triptych,*
Adoration of the Magi,
The Nativity *and*
The Circumcision of Christ.
Panel, 131 × 90 cm (centre panel)
and 131 × 35 cm (wings).
Whereabouts unknown.

sixteenth century, many town halls, particularly in Germany, were decorated with series of paintings portraying women's wiles.[6] Such images encouraged lawful marriage by displaying examples of immorality. This lends strength to the theory that the Solomon triptych was a gift at the wedding of Willem Simonz and Adriana van Duyveland in 1521, a gift intended to foster marital fidelity.

As there is no precedent for this combination of king Solomon paintings, it may be assumed that the work was commissioned for the wedding. For the open market a painter would have produced more standard, and thus more saleable, pictures.

For a long time this triptych was the only extant painting by the anonymous Master of the Solomon Triptych. However, in 1988, a second triptych surfaced at an auction (fig. 3). Friedländer had already attributed this work to the same artist before its disappearance.[7] Points of similarity in this second work are the elongated, elegant figures, their clothing draped over the floor, their rather broad faces with fine features, the fantastical architecture and the little dog. Since there can be no doubt that Friedländer was correct in his attribution, the œuvre of the Master of the Solomon Triptych now comprises two known works. This artist may be considered one of the Antwerp Mannerists, a group of artists who worked in the second and third decade of the sixteenth century. Their paintings were characterized by such features as the elegant poses of the figures in luxuriously draped robes, fanciful architecture and use of vivid colours.[8] The elegant figures, viewed from the rear, on the centre and right panels of the Solomon triptych are typical of this school. Should another work by this master be re-discovered, it could be identified immediately from the distinctive faces with their wide-set eyes, narrow mouths and curiously folded ears.

TECHNICAL ASPECTS *The frames on the wings are original but the painted decoration has been lost. The inner moulding of the frames on the inside of the triptych was gilded; around the exterior panels the inner moulding was originally painted green.*

There is extensive underdrawing in brush which is also clearly visible to the naked eye (infrared reflectography by P. van den Brink and M. Baldin, 1992).[9] The interior of the triptych is in excellent state of preservation.[10] In 1967 the interior of the triptych was cleaned; in 1996 restoration of the exterior panels was completed.

PROVENANCE *Collection of Willem Simonz, lord of Stavenisse and Zierikzee (1498-1557); by descent, Jonkheer J. de Witte van Citters collection, The Hague; in 1876 bequeathed to the State of the Netherlands for display in the Mauritshuis; inv.no. 433.*

LITERATURE *Friedländer 1967-76, XI (1974), pp. 35, 73, no. 64; Tóth-Ubbens 1968, pp. 35-36; Broos, 1993, no. 43 (with further literature); Van den Brink 1997, no. 21.*

1 See: Broos 1993, pp. 357-59.
2 From his small series on the theme of women's tricks, dated *c.*1517. Hollstein 1996, pp. 164-70, nos. 181-86 (the woodcut shown here is no. 184/1).
3 Vignau Wilberg-Schuurman 1983, figs 55 and 56.
4 With its 'two cherubim of olive tree' (upper centre, 1 Kings 6:23), 'carved figures of cherubim and palm trees and open flowers' (1 Kings 6:29) and 'two pillars of brass' (1 Kings 7:15).
5 See: Hollstein 1996, pp. 58-59, no. 30. This engraving is based in its turn on a rendering of this subject from 1504 by the German Master MZ. See: Vignau Wilberg-Schuurman 1983, fig. 55. Tóth-Ubbens 1968, p. 36, pointed out the connection between this work and the prints of Lucas van Leyden.
6 Vignau Wilberg-Schuurman 1983, p. 49 ff.
7 Friedländer 1967-76, XI (1973), no. 65 (no fig.). It was auctioned at Christie's in New York on 15 January 1988 (lot 93). Peter van den Brink was kind enough to bring this to my attention. I consider two other side panels, which Friedländer also attributed to this master (no. 66), to be by another artist.
8 Compare, for example, the work of the Master of the Antwerp Adoration: Friedländer 1967-76, XI (1974), nos. 46-58; no. 52 in particular bears a great resemblance to fig. 3, and the work of the Master of the Groote Adoration, for example no. 27.
9 Van den Brink 1997, no. 21, describes the underdrawing as consistent with the Antwerp style of underdrawing in that period.
10 For a technical description see: Broos 1993, p. 358.

8   UNKNOWN PAINTER AND SCULPTOR FROM HAARLEM

Triptych with The Crucifixion and Scenes of the Passion, c.1490-1500

Exterior panels: *The Holy Kindred*
Panel and polychrome wood carving, 91 × 44 cm
(when closed) and 70 × 22 cm (wings)
Private collection

When open this beautiful triptych from the late fifteenth century comprises a carved wood crucifixion group and painted wings with scenes of Christ's Passion. When closed, a continuous painting on the exterior panels depicts the Holy Kindred. The modest dimensions of this work suggest that it was intended for private devotion. Such a piece, combining painting and sculpture from the Northern Netherlands in this period, is extremely rare.

The presence of Mary, with her hands clasped in sorrow, and John the Evangelist at the foot of the Cross, is drawn from a passage in the New Testament, in which the crucified Christ entrusts his mother to the care of his

favourite disciple (John 19:26-27). Although not mentioned by name, this disciple has been traditionally identified as John. On the interior of the wings are scenes of Christ's Passion. Six different scenes run into each other through ingenious use of architectural and landscape elements. Upper left is Christ praying on the Mount of Olives while an angel appears with a cross. Judas enters through the gate with a pouch of money, followed by the soldiers who will arrest Christ. The chalice on the mountain echoes Christ's plea for the cup (of sacrificial death) to be taken from him (Matthew 26:39, 42; Mark 14:36). The presence of the chalice, which is shaped like a com-

munion cup, is also a reference to the sacrifice of the Mass. Below this scene the Flagellation of Christ is depicted, while lower left is the Crowning with Thorns. In the scenes of the passion on the right wing, Mary always plays a role. She can be recognized from her blue mantle and white wimple. Through her grief and 'compassion' for Christ, she served as an important model for the faithful who were supposed to empathize with Christ's suffering.[1] In the Cross Bearing at the upper right she looks on, while in the middle scene she holds her Son's head in her lap. This is the moment when she laments the death of Christ, following his Deposition from the Cross.[2] John kneels beside Mary. The Cross is shown to the extreme left, with the Instruments of the Passion, the crown of thorns and crucifixion nails at its foot. In the Entombment scene, depicted lower right, Mary Magdalene kisses the hand of Christ.

The painting on the exterior panels represents the Holy Kindred, which comprises Mary with Child, Joseph and Mary's parents, Anne and Joachim.[3] The picture contains many symbolic motifs. For example, Mary, her Child and her mother are sitting in an enclosed garden, the *hortus conclusus* from the Song of Solomon (Song of Solomon 4:12-15), which symbolizes Mary's virginity.[4] The Song of Solomon was interpreted by Bernard of Clairvaux (1090-1153) as an allegory with Mary as the bride. Other symbols of Mary derived from the Song of Solomon are the white lily which Joseph is handing to her over the little wall, and 'David's Tower' in the background (Song of Solomon 2:2, 4:4). Mary is seated on the ground which alludes to her humility.[5] The daisy which the Child is handing to Anne symbolizes Christ's incarnation, while the red carnations on the grassy bank are another attribute of Mary: the red colour alludes to divine love.[6] The peacocks as a Christian symbol are possibly a reference to Christ's Resurrection.[7] In the background landscape a figure with a wide-brimmed hat rides on a white horse. This rider may represent James the Greater, the son of Mary's half-sister Mary Salome, who also belongs to the Holy Kindred.[8]

These paintings show similarity in style and composition to the work of Geertgen tot Sint-Jans (1460/65-c.1495) and his followers, such as the Master of the Brunswick Diptych (active c.1490), probably indicating that this triptych was produced in Haarlem around 1490-1500. The Lamentation on the right panel, for example, is a variation on Geertgen's renowned model, now in Vienna (see p. 7, fig. 1) The finely painted faces, which are in good condition on the right panel, also recall work by Geertgen tot Sint-Jans. The stylistic affinity with the Master of the Brunswick Diptych is illustrated by his diptych showing St Anne, the Virgin and Child with a Carthusian donor in Brunswick (fig. 1).[9] The similarities in composition, and also in details – for example the vegetation in the foreground – are striking.

A piece which combines sculpture and painting is generally the product of collaboration between a sculptor, a painter who also polychromed the wood carving, and a cabinet-maker who provided the frame for the paintings and a cabinet for the sculpture. Around 1500, the production of altarpieces which combined wood carving with painted panels expanded enormously in the Southern Netherlands, following a German altarpiece tradition which had already begun to flourish in the fourteenth century. Antwerp workshops produced many imposing altarpieces which were often intended for export.[10] However, production of such pieces never spread to the Northern Netherlands. Attribution of the paintings on this triptych to a Haarlem master could prove significant to the history of sculpture, if the supposition is correct that not only the paintings but also the entire triptych was made in Haarlem. For there is virtually no sculpture from this period which is indisputably known to have been made in a town or city in Holland (the present Dutch provinces of Noord and Zuid Holland).[11]

TECHNICAL ASPECTS *The cross, the pilasters, the corner ornaments and the hill of Golgotha in the sculpture group are not original. It is also possible that the pedestal and ornamental border at the top of the cabinet and wings were not part of the original structure. The triptych was restored in 1995.*

PROVENANCE *Auction Monaco (Christie's), 30 June 1995, lot 10 (as Circle of the Master of the Brunswick Diptych).*

1 This was mainly propagated by followers of the Devotio Moderna (Modern Devotion). See: Caron 1984.
2 The theme of the Lamentation has its origins in mystical writings from the thirteenth and fourteenth centuries. See: Hall 1979, pp. 246-47.
3 For the tradition of Holy Kindred images, see cat. 10.
4 In his *Speculum humanae salvationis* (1324), Ludolph of Saxony also interprets the enclosed garden as a symbol of Mary's Immaculate Conception in her mother's womb. See also: Muller 1985, pp. 84-85.
5 Compare Meiss 1936.
6 See Levi d'Ancona 1977 for the daisy, pp. 124-26, and the red carnation, pp. 79-84.
7 Hall 1979, p. 238.
8 For James the Greater as member of the Holy Kindred, see cat. 10.
9 The similarity between the triptych here displayed and the work of the Master of the Brunswick Diptych was first commented on by E. Buijsen in auction catalogue Monaco (Christie's), 30 June 1995, p. 13. For this master see: Châtelet 1980, pp. 124-33, Friedländer 1967-76, v (1969), nos. 16-21. Identification of the Master of the Brunswick Diptych with Jacob Jansz, the master of Jan Mostaert, as proposed in: Amsterdam 1958, pp. 55-56, and elaborated by Châtelet, remains a hypothesis.
10 See Antwerp 1993.
11 With thanks to Frits Scholten, Rijksmuseum, Amsterdam.

9 MASTER OF ALKMAAR (ACTIVE c.1500)

Willem Jelysz van Soutelande and Kathrijn van der Graft Willemsdr with family members and the Saints James the Greater and Mary Magdalene, c.1515

Reverse: escutcheons with coats of arms
Panel, 102 × 36 cm (each)
Rijksmuseum, Amsterdam

Originally these panels with praying donors and saints formed the side wings of a triptych whose central section, with a scene from the Bible or of saints, has been lost. On the back of the panels, escutcheons bearing the coats of arms of the Van Soutelande and Van der Graft families are depicted in a trompe l'oeil fashion, hanging from leather straps in stone niches. These arms also feature on the interior panels where they appear as decoration on the prie-dieus. Probably this triptych was made for an altar which was raised by the couple portrayed in the painting, close to the family grave, that may have been located in the St Bavo Church in Haarlem.[1] After the Reformation such altar pieces were generally returned to the family, if they had survived the Iconoclastic Fury. Families were often anxious to purge such works of their now undesirable 'popish' elements; the panels here displayed may well have been separated from the central section during this period.[2] The wings, whose upper edges were originally partially rounded, were turned into rectangles, thereby diluting the memory of the original triptych still further. No longer an altarpiece or a memorial piece,[3] the work became a family portrait whose two extant components shared an integral frame at the time of their purchase by the Rijksmuseum in 1885.[4]

As was the custom, the gentlemen were depicted on the left wing, in the position of precedence on the right-hand side of the scene on the centre panel. One of the figures is a monk, who can be recognized from his tonsure. Five of the ladies on the right wing are dressed in religious habits. The armoured knight has been identified from his coat of arms as Willem Jelysz van Soutelande, who was sheriff of Haarlem a number of times.[5] The original triptych may well have been commissioned on his death in 1515 or 1516, to keep alive the memory of himself

and his family at his grave. The palm branch against his shoulder is a so-called Jerusalem feather, and indicates that he belonged to the Knightly Brotherhood of the Holy Land: he had therefore undertaken a pilgrimage to Jerusalem and the holy sepulchre.[6] Facing him on the right panel kneels his wife Kathrijn Willemsdr van der Graft, to whom he had only been married a few years when she died in 1490 or 1491.[7] They had just one son, who is presumably depicted behind his father. The other figures in the painting undoubtedly belong to the donors' families. The second boy from the left beneath James the Greater's sleeve, and the girl to the extreme left on the right panel, are later additions.[8]

The coat of arms on the escutcheon held by a flying angel on the right panel is identical to the arms of the Van der Graft family. However, this particular coat of arms was also borne by other families. The genealogist M. Thierry de Bye Dólleman has connected these arms on the upper right with the Van Waveren family of Haarlem:[9] in 1484 Margriet van Waveren married Jacob de Wael van Rozenburg (died 1524) who bore the beheaded lion coat of arms that appears on the escutcheon upper left.[10] Since it is unlikely that unrelated families would have jointly commissioned such a work, there must have been a connection between the Van Soutelande-Van der Graft and De Wael-Van Waveren couples – if Thierry de Bye Dólleman's surmise is correct.

On the original triptych, the saints who accompanied the donors acted as intercessors, putting in a good word for the pious family with Christ, Mary or any saint who might have featured on the centre panel. James the Greater can be recognized from his staff and pilgrim's hat with scallop shells, Mary Magdalene from her jar of ointment. Although James may have been included as the

name saint of Jacob de Wael, it is also possible that James the Greater and Mary Magdalene were family saints, or that the altar for which this piece was painted was dedicated to them.[11]

Reconstruction of the œuvre of the Master of Alkmaar is based on a work from 1504, which comprises seven panels with scenes illustrating the Works of Charity (including fig. 1). Until 1918 this ensemble was kept in the St Laurence Church in Alkmaar from which the anonymous painter has acquired his name. He worked in Alkmaar and Haarlem, and must have been a contemporary of Geertgen tot Sint-Jans (1460/65-c.1495).[12] Similarity in the rendering of figures, such as the finely drawn faces with almond-shaped eyes, justify the traditional attribution of the paintings here displayed to the Master of Alkmaar. However, if the fluid painting of the distant landscape in the background is compared with the stone-by-stone rendering of the architecture of the charity panels, attribution of this landscape element to one and the same painter seems scarcely tenable. It is possible that the Master of Alkmaar entrusted painting of the background landscape to a colleague who was specialized in this genre.

1 *Master of Alkmaar,* Clothing the Naked, *1504. Panel, 101 × 55.5 cm. Rijksmuseum, Amsterdam.*

TECHNICAL ASPECTS *The corners upper right (on the left panel) and upper left (on the right panel) are later additions; presumably the panels were originally half rounded.*

Several pentimenti can be seen with the naked eye. The most important of these is on the left panel where the second man (with the fur collar) behind the prie-dieu, originally wore the same armour as the knight in the foreground. The knight's coat of mail is a later addition by the painter (with thanks to Manja Zeldenrust, Rijksmuseum, Amsterdam).

PROVENANCE *F. Gael-van Leyden Collection?, Leiden;[13] auction, L.H. van der Hoop Tilanus, The Hague, 1885 (date unknown); inv.no. Sk-A-1188.*

LITERATURE *Jaarverslag Rijks Museum van Schilderijen (Annual Report) 1885, p. 55; Van Gelder-Schrijver, 1930, pp. 108-10; Hoogewerff 1936-47, II (1937), pp. 378-80; Thierry de Bye Dólleman 1965, pp. 1-8; Friedländer 1967-76, X (1973), no. 53; Van Thiel et al. 1976, pp. 628-29; Heller, 1976, no. 154.*

1 Given the donors' Haarlem background, Thierry de Bye Dólleman (1965, p. 6) suggests that the altarpiece was intended for this church.

2 See Bok 1996, in particular pp. 222-25.

3 A memorial piece, intended to commemorate the depicted donors, was generally provided with a text on a separate panel. This would state who were the depicted persons, and the reader was besought to pray for their souls. The majority of these text panels have been lost. See: Defoer 1996. It is possible that such a text panel originally accompanied the work under discussion.

4 See Jaarverslag Rijks Museum van Schilderijen (Annual Report) 1885, p. 55. The present frames are probably sixteenth-century northern European (French) and were remodelled to fit the panels. The slats securing the frames suggest that this was done in the present century (with thanks to Hubert Baya, Rijksmuseum, Amsterdam).

5 For identification of the figures see: Thierry de Bye Dólleman 1965, pp. 1-8.

6 Thierry de Bye Dólleman 1965, p. 3, partly bases his identification on Jan van Scorel's group portrait of the Haarlem Jerusalem Crusaders from 1527-1529, in which Van Soutelande is depicted (Frans Halsmuseum, Haarlem, inv.no. 263). He came from a family which wrongfully claimed descent from the first counts of Holland (see Thierry de Bye Dólleman 1965, p. 2, 7).

7 In 1486 Van Soutelande was still unmarried and living with his mother. See Thierry de Bye Dólleman 1965, p. 5.

8 Hoogewerff's suggestion (1936-47, II, p. 380) that the upper section, with the landscapes, angels and saints, has been added is untenable.

9 Thierry de Bye Dólleman 1965, pp. 2-3.

10 Thierry de Bye Dólleman suggests that this couple may have been portrayed on the lost central panel, and that several of their children may appear on the side panels. The couple depicted next to Van Soutelande and his wife behind the prie-dieus are probably not De Wael and Van Waveren, as the woman is wearing a religious habit: Margriet van Waveren could only have assumed such a habit after the death of her husband in 1524, while the panels presumably date from the second decade of the sixteenth century.

11 Compare Heller 1976, pp. 49-50.

12 See Bruyn 1966, p. 224; De Bruyn Kops 1975, pp. 203-05; G. Lemmens in Friedländer 1967-76, X (1973), pp. 90-91.

13 Van Gelder-Schrijver 1930, p. 109, note 2: as 'previously in the possession of the Leyden Gael family of Leiden'. For the F. Gael-van Leyden Collection see: J.P. Filedt Kok in Amsterdam 1978, pp. 7-8. The Van de Graft family was also called Gael. Compare the *Portrait of Dirckje Gael, called van der Graft* by Pieter Pietersz, 1588 (Rijksmuseum, inv.no. Sk-A-3865, Van Thiel et al., 1976, p. 446).

10   HANS SUESS VON KULMBACH (*c.*1480-1522)

a   *Mary Salome and her family,* 1513
b   *Mary Cleophas and her family, c.*1513

Panel, 55 × 28 cm (each)
Mauritshuis, The Hague

84

1 Hans Suess von Kulmbach,
The Annunciation to Joachim
(originally on the reverse of
Mary Salome). *Panel, 55 × 28 cm.*
Whereabouts unknown (photo,
Max J. Friedländer Archive,
Netherlands Institute for Art
History, The Hague).

2 Hans Suess von Kulmbach,
St Anne and Joachim at the
Golden Gate *(originally on the*
reverse of Mary Cleophas). *Panel,*
55 × 28 cm. Barnes Foundation
Museum, Merion, Pennsylvania
(photo, Max J. Friedländer
Archive, Netherlands Institute
for Art History, The Hague).

These paintings by Hans Suess von Kulmbach, who worked in Nuremberg, depict Mary's two half-sisters with their husbands and children. Until recently it was not known that the panels had been sawn through in the past, separating the painted front and reverse sides. One of the sawn-off outside panels is presently kept in the Barnes Foundation, in Merion, Pennsylvania; the location of the other one is unknown (figs 1 and 2).[1] In 1925 the four panels – that were apparently already sawn apart at that time – were still together in the collection of Count von Cauda in Berlin. Shortly afterwards, however, the panels now in The Hague were sold as a pair.

The original reverse sides of the panels show the annunciation to Joachim and the meeting of St Anne and Joachim at the Golden Gate. Undoubtedly these four paintings belonged to an altarpiece that was dedicated to St Anne, the mother of Mary, and her descendants: the Holy Kindred. During the fifteenth century the cult of St Anne, who was not included in the official Roman Catholic calendar of saints until 1481, expanded enormously, particularly in the Rhineland and the Low Countries.[2] In northern Europe St Anne with the Virgin and the Christ Child and the Holy Kindred enjoyed great popularity as subjects of altarpieces.

Attention was first drawn to Jesus' grandmother in the Gospels of the Apocrypha and over the centuries St Anne's life was expanded with all kinds of legends, including the one of her three marriages. After the death of Joachim she was believed to have married another two times; the daughters from each of these marriages, both of whom were called Mary like their famous half-sister, are depicted on these panels with their families in domestic scenes. St Anne's second daughter Mary Cleophas was married to Alphaeus and bore him four sons, three of

whom would become apostles. They can be recognized from their martyr's attributes: to the left Judas Thaddaeus (St Jude) with a club, in the centre James the Less with a fuller's staff, to the right Simon the Zealot with a saw and in the background Joseph the Righteous (without attribute). Mary Cleophas is brushing the hair of her oldest child and Alphaeus is depicted as a caring father with the youngest. The primer with imaginary Hebrew letters which Simon holds probably alludes to his later role as a preacher of the Gospel. The other Mauritshuis painting represents St Anne's youngest daughter, Mary Salome, who raised two children with her husband Zebedee: the apostles James the Greater with his staff and shoulder bag, and John the Evangelist with his chalice, here being breastfed by his mother. Their father is depicted writing, a reference to his fatherly role as teacher.

The painting on the back of the Mary Salome panel was *The Annunciation to Joachim* (fig. 1), while the painting behind Mary Cleophas was *St Anne and Joachim at the Golden Gate* (fig. 2), both events which preceded Mary's birth. Joachim had withdrawn with his flock of sheep, in a state of despair as Anne was advanced in years and still childless. An angel urged him to return, and the couple met at the Golden Gate of Jerusalem; nine months later Mary was born.

Unfortunately the exact construction of this dismantled altarpiece by Suess von Kulmbach cannot be construed as only these four paintings have survived. It might have had wings each consisting of two panels, one mounted above the other.[3] The original ensemble probably comprised a comprehensive portrait of the Holy Kindred, including scenes of St Anne with her various husbands, and of St Anne with her daughters. Presumably the Christ Child, the most important scion of St Anne's

3 Lucas Cranach the Elder, The Holy Kindred, 1509. Panel, 120 × 99 cm (centre panel) and 120 × 43.5 cm (wings). Städelsches Kunstinstitut, Frankfurt.

family, occupied a central position in this altarpiece, perhaps in a scene showing St Anne and the Virgin Mary. The paintings in the Mauritshuis would have been positioned on the inside wings of such an altarpiece, while the scenes preceding Mary's birth were probably painted on the exterior wings. When closed *The Annunciation to Joachim* would have been placed to the left of *Anna and Joachim at the Golden Gate* as paintings which told a story were supposed to be read from left to right. Mary Salome and her family, who are represented on the reverse side of *The Annunciation to Joachim,* would therefore have been seen to the left of Mary Cleophas when the altarpiece was opened. However, this conflicts with the chronological order, since Anne's third daughter (Mary Salome) then appears before her second daughter (Mary Cleophas).

Nevertheless, the composition of the painting in the Mauritshuis confirms this original order because in this way the two sisters are turning towards each other.

It is not known for which church or cloister Suess von Kulmbach's dismantled and partially lost altarpiece of 1513 was originally intended. However, there are several documented examples of brotherhoods devoted to the cult of St Anne who commissioned altarpieces for their chapel or cloister. Around 1500 the Brotherhood of St Anne in Frankfurt commissioned a retable with sixteen paintings from a Brussels master for the Carmelite cloister in Frankfurt.[4] In 1507 the St Anne Brotherhood of Louvain commissioned a triptych depicting the Holy Kindred of St Anne for their altar in St Peter's Church. This altarpiece was completed in 1509 by Quinten Matsys

4 Hans Suess von Kulmbach,
Mary Salome and her Family.
Panel 58,1 × 33,2 cm. City Art
Museum, Saint Louis.

(1465/66-1530). St Anne was also popular in noble circles. Lucas Cranach the Elder (1472-1553), court painter to Frederick the Wise, Elector of Saxony, painted a triptych with the Holy Kindred for his patron in 1509, destined for the St Mary's Church in Torgau (fig. 3).[5] Suess von Kulmbach appears to have been inspired by this triptych which features Mary Cleophas and Mary Salome on the wings. He may well have derived the domestic motifs of breastfeeding a baby and brushing a child's hair from this work.[6]

Although Hans Suess, who came from Kulmbach, only acquired citizenship of Nuremberg in 1511, he was working in this city well before 1500, and was probably apprenticed to Albrecht Dürer (1471-1528). From 1511, when Suess apparently set up as an independent master, his production can be followed from year to year through dated works. While his fellow townsman Dürer concentrated on graphic work and major commissions for the emperor, Suess specialized in the production of altarpieces and portraits.[7] As a draughtsman he focused on the design of stained-glass windows. One painting produced by Suess von Kulmbach, now in St Louis, Illinois, probably formed part of a similar St Anne altar piece.[8] It is a free variation on the composition of Mary Salome and her family (fig. 4).

TECHNICAL ASPECTS *Both panels were originally painted on both sides but were sawn apart. Old photos have been used in order to establish that the companion paintings are those shown in figs 1 and 2. The characteristic wood grain, visible on the unpainted edges of the Mauritshuis panels, corresponds to the grain on the panels shown in figs 1 and 2. The paintings in the Mauritshuis, which were planed down to a thickness of two to three millimetres, have been cradled.*

A fluent, sketchy underdrawing in brush is visible to the naked eye. Several minor deviations from this underdrawing can be detected in the painting. The colours were originally vivid. The paint surface is now fairly worn (probably largely due to incorrect cleaning), allowing the light-coloured ground to shine through more than was originally intended. The paintings were restored in 1996.

PROVENANCE *Count von Cauda Collection, Berlin, 1925, (with the paintings shown in figs 1 and 2); art dealers J. Böhler, Lucerne; art dealers H. Perl, Berlin or Paris; art dealers J. Goudstikker, Amsterdam, 1928; Stichting Nederlands Kunstbezit, 1945; from 1951 on loan to the Maurithuis; since 1960 owned by the Mauritshuis; inv.nos. 904-905.*

LITERATURE *Berlin 1925, no. 208 (with the paintings shown in figs 1 and 2); Stadler 1936, no. 72; Winkler 1959, p. 69; Broos 1993, p. 366, fig. 2.*

1 See also Technical aspects. It was already known that these four paintings once formed part of the same polyptych. See Stadler 1936, no. 72.
2 For the cult of St Anne in the Netherlands and Rhineland in the fifteenth and sixteenth centuries see: Brandenbarg 1985, Brandenbarg 1990 and Uden 1992.
3 Compare Stadler 1936, no. 63.
4 Brandenbarg 1985, pp. 114-117; Uden 1992, pp. 60-64.
5 Friedländer/Roosenberg 1978, no. 18; Uden 1992, pp. 70-72.
6 Compare a popular print by Lucas Cranach the Elder in which Mary Cleophas is also breastfeeding her baby, while her husband teaches the other children to read. Uden 1992, pp. 74-75.
7 For Suess von Kulmbach see e.g.: Stadler 1936, Winkler 1959, Butts 1985.
8 Stadler 1936, no. 71.

BIBLIOGRAPHY

AINSWORTH 1989 M.W. Ainsworth, 'Northern Renaissance Drawings and Underdrawings: A Proposed Method of Study', *Master Drawings* XXVII (1989), pp. 5-38

AINSWORTH 1990 M.W. Ainsworth, 'Book review of Hans J. van Miegroet, *Gerard David, 1989*', *Art Bulletin* LXXII (1990), no. 4, pp. 649-54

AINSWORTH 1994a M.W. Ainsworth, 'Gerard David', in: R. Van Schoute, B. De Patoul (eds), *Les Primitifs flamands et leur temps,* Louvain 1994, pp. 482-93

AINSWORTH 1994b M.W. Ainsworth, 'Hans Memling as a draughtsman', in: Bruges 1994, pp. 78-81

ALLEN/GARDNER 1954 J.L. Allen, E.E. Gardner, *A concise catalogue of the European paintings in the Metropolitan Museum of Art,* New York 1954

AMSTERDAM 1958 *Middeleeuwse kunst der Noordelijke Nederlanden,* Amsterdam (Rijksmuseum), 1958

AMSTERDAM 1978 J.P. Filedt Kok, *Lucas van Leyden – grafiek (1498 of 1494-1533),* Amsterdam (Rijksprentenkabinet), 1978

AMSTERDAM 1994-95 H.W. van Os, *The Art of Devotion in the Late Middle Ages in Europe 1300-1500,* Amsterdam (Rijksmuseum), 1994-95

AMSTERDAM/BOSTON/PHILADELPHIA 1987-88 P.C. Sutton et al., *Masters of 17th-Century Dutch Landscape Painting,* Amsterdam (Rijksmuseum), Boston (Museum of Fine Arts), Philadelphia (Philadelphia Museum of Art), 1987-88

ANTWERP 1930 *Exposition Internationale Coloniale Maritime et d'Art Flamand. Section d'Art Flamand Ancien. Tôme 1er. Peinture – Dessins – Tapisseries,* Antwerp 1930

ANTWERP 1993 H. Nieuwdorp (ed.), *Antwerpse retabels 15de-16de eeuw,* Antwerp (Cathedral), 1993

AXTERS 1950-60 S. Axters, *Geschiedenis van de Vroomheid in de Nederlanden,* I-IV, Antwerp 1950-60

BAETJER 1980 K. Baetjer, *European Paintings in The Metropolitan Museum of Art by artists born in or before 1865,* I-III, New York 1980

BAETJER 1995 K. Baetjer, *European Paintings in The Metropolitan Museum of Art by artists born before 1865. A summary catalogue,* New York 1995

BALDASS 1936 L. Baldass, 'Gerard David als Landschaftsmaler', *Jahrbuch der Kunsthistorischen Sammlungen in Wien* N.F. X (1936), pp. 89-96

BAUMAN 1986 G. Bauman, 'Early Flemish Portraits 1425-1525', *The Metropolitan Museum of Art Bulletin* XLII (1986), no. 4, pp. 1-64

BAUMAN ET AL. 1992 G.C. Bauman, W.A. Liedtke, H. Vlieghe (eds), *Flemish Paintings in America,* Antwerp 1992

BAX 1979 D. Bax, *Hieronymus Bosch, his picture-writing deciphered,* Rotterdam 1979

BEHLING 1967 L. Behling, *Die Pflanze in der frühen älterlichen Tafelmalerei,* Cologne 1967

BELTING/KRUSE 1994 H. Belting, C. Kruse, *Die Erfindung des Gemäldes. Das erste Jahrhundert der niederländischen Malerei,* Munich 1994

BERLIN 1925 *Gemälde alter Meister aus berliner Besitz,* Berlin (Akademie der Künste), 1925

BIAŁOSTOCKI 1966 J. Białostocki, *Les Primitifs Flamands. Les musées de Pologne,* Brussels 1966

BIBLE IN DUYTSCHE 1477 *Bible in duytsche,* I-II, Delft (Jacob Jacobsz van der Meer, Mauricius Yemantszoon), 1477

BIERITZ 1988 K.-H. Bieritz, *Das Kirchenjahr. Feste, Gedenk- und Feiertage in Geschichte und Gegenwart,* Munich 1988

BOK 1996 M.J. Bok, 'Laying claims to nobility in the Dutch republic: epitaphs, true and false', *Simiolus* XXIV (1996), pp. 209-26

BONAVENTURA S. Bonaventura, *Opera Omnia* VII, Quaracchi 1895

BOON 1946 K.G. Boon, *Gerard David,* Amsterdam [1946]

BRANDENBARG 1985 T. Brandenbarg, 'St.-Anna en haar familie. De Anna-verering in verband met opvattingen over huwelijk en gezin in de vroeg-moderne tijd', in: Nijmegen 1985, pp. 101-27

BRANDENBARG 1990 T. Brandenbarg, *Heilig familieleven. Verspreiding en waardering van de Historie van Sint-Anna in de stedelijke cultuur in de Nederlanden en het Rijnland aan het begin van de moderne tijd (15de/16de eeuw)*, Nijmegen 1990

BRAUN 1924 J. Braun, *Der Christliche Altar in seiner geschichtlichen Entwicklung*, I-II, Munich 1924

BREDIUS 1895 A. Bredius, *Musée royal de la Haye (Mauritshuis). Catalogue raisonné des tableaux et sculptures*, The Hague 1895

BRINK 1997 P. van den Brink, *Ondertekening en andere technische aspecten van de Antwerpse maniëristen 1500-1525*, forthcoming 1997

BRÖKER 1995 P. Bröker, *Rondom kerstmis. Iconografie en symboliek in de beeldende kunst rondom de geboorte van Christus*, Utrecht 1995

BROOS 1987 B. Broos, *Meesterwerken in het Mauritshuis*, The Hague 1987

BROOS 1988 B. Broos, *Guide, Mauritshuis, The Hague*, The Hague 1988

BROOS 1993 B. Broos, *Intimacies & Intrigues. History Painting in the Mauritshuis*, The Hague/Ghent 1993

BRUGES 1949 *Gerard David*, Bruges (Stedelijk Museum), 1949

BRUGES 1984 P. Huvenne, *Pierre Pourbus: Peintre Brugeois 1524-1584*, Bruges (Memlingmuseum), 1984

BRUGES 1994 *Hans Memling*, Bruges (Groeningemuseum), 1994

BRUGES/LOUVAIN-LA-NEUVE 1985 I. Vandevivere, *Juan de Flandes*, Bruges (Memlingmuseum), Louvain-la-Neuve (Musée universitaire), 1985

BRUSSELS 1935 *Cinq siècles d'art*, Brussels (Exposition universelle et international), 1935

BRUSSELS 1953 *Bruxelles au xve siècle*, Brussels (Musée Communal), 1953

BRUSSELS 1977 *Albrecht Dürer in de Nederlanden, zijn reis (1520-1521) en invloed*, Brussels (Palais des Beaux-Arts), 1977

BRUYN 1966 J. Bruyn, 'De Abdij van Egmond als opdrachtgeefster van kunstwerken in het begin van de zestiende eeuw', *Oud Holland* LXXXI (1966), pp. 145-72, 197-227

DE BRUYN KOPS 1975 C.J. de Bruyn Kops, 'De Zeven Werken van Barmhartigheid van de Meester van Alkmaar gerestaureerd', *Bulletin van het Rijksmuseum* XXIII (1975), pp. 203-26

BUIJSEN 1986 E. Buijsen, *De ikonografie van de heilige Antonius van Padua in de Vlaamse schilderkunst vóór de contra-reformatie* (typescript), Leiden 1986

BUIJSEN 1996 E. Buijsen, 'A Rediscovered Wing of a Diptych by Hans Memling (c. 1440-1494)', *Oud Holland* CX (1996), pp. 57-69

BURROUGHS 1945 L. Burroughs, 'Notes', *The Metropolitan Museum of Art Bulletin* IV (1945), facing p. 97

BURROWS 1930 C. Burrows, 'Letter from New York', *Apollo* XI (1930), pp. 449-52

BUTTS 1985 B.R. Butts, *'Dürerschüler' Hans Süss von Kulmbach*, Ann Arbor 1985

BUTZKAMM 1990 A. Butzkamm, *Bild und Frömmigkeit im 15. Jahrhundert. Der Sakramentsaltar von Dieric Bouts in der St.-Peterskirche zu Löwen*, Paderborn 1990

CAMPBELL 1976 L. Campbell, 'The Art Market in the Southern Netherlands in the fifteenth century', *Burlington Magazine* CXVIII (1976), pp. 188-98

CARON 1984 M.L. Caron, 'Ansien doet gedencken. De religieuze voorstellingswereld van de Moderne Devotie', in: *Geert Grote en de Moderne Devotie*, Deventer (De Waag), Utrecht (Rijksmuseum Het Catharijneconvent), 1984

VAN DE CASTYNE 1935 O. Van de Castyne, 'Autour de "l'instruction pastorale" du Louvre', *Revue Belge d'Architecture et d'Histoire de l'Art* V (1935), pp. 319-28

VAN DE CASTYNE 1936 O. Van de Castyne, 'Autour de l'instruction pastorale du Louvre, Saint Augustin ou Saint Géry?', *Revue Belge d'Architecture et d'Histoire de l'Art* VI (1936), pp. 63-65

CAT. AMSTERDAM 1934 *Catalogus der Schilderijen, Pastels, Miniaturen, Aquarellen, tentoongesteld in het Rijksmuseum*, Amsterdam 1934

CAT. BACHE 1929 *A Catalogue of Paintings in the Collection of Jules S. Bache*, New York 1929

CAT. BACHE 1944 *A Catalogue of Paintings in the Bache Collection. The Metropolitan Museum of Art*, New York 1944

CAT. BERLIN 1975 *Katalog der ausgestellten Gemälde des 13.-18. Jahrhunderts*, Berlin (Staatliche Museen zu Berlin, Gemäldegalerie), 1975

CAT. DUVEEN 1941 *Duveen Pictures in Public Collections of America*, New York 1941

CHÂTELET 1980 A. Châtelet, *Les Primitifs hollandais. La peinture dans les Pays-Bas du Nord au xve siècle*, Paris/Freiburg 1980

CLEMENS OF ALEXANDRIA *Des Clemens von Alexandreia, Bibliothek des Kirchenväter II, Bd. 19*, Munich 1937

CLEVEN 1990 E. Cleven, '"Ach, was ist der Wald schön grün" Gerard David, das 'bosgezicht' und sein (Miss-)Verständnis', *Akt* XLVI (1990), pp. 2-14

COCKSHAW 1979 P. Cockshaw, *Les miniatures des chroniques de Hainaut*, n.p. 1979

COMPTON 1958-59 M. Compton, 'A Triptych by The Master of Frankfurt', *The Liverpool Libraries, Museum & Arts Committee Bulletin* VII (1958-59), no. 3, pp. 5-17

CORPUS CHRISTIANORUM 1959 *Corpus Christianorum. Series Latina LXXII. S. Hieronymi Presbyteri Opera. Pars 1. Opera Exegetica 1*, Turnhout 1959

CORPUS CHRISTIANORUM 1963 *Corpus Christianorum. Series Latina LXXIII, S. Hieronymi Presbyteri Opera. Pars 1. Opera Exegetica 2. Commentariorium in Esaiam. Libr. 1-XI*, Turnhout 1963

CORTISSOZ 1930 R. Cortissoz, 'The Jules S. Bache Collection', *American Magazine of Art* XXI (1930), pp. 243-59

COURCELLE 1965-72 J. Courcelle, P. Courcelle, *Iconographie de Saint Augustin*, I-III, Paris 1965-72

CUTTLER 1968 C.D. Cuttler, *Northern Painting. From Pucelle to Bruegel. Fourteenth, Fifteenth, and Sixteenth Centuries*, New York etc. 1968

DEFOER 1996 H.L.M. Defoer, 'Volledige memorietafels zeldzaam in museaal bezit', *Vereniging Rembrandt. Nationaal Fonds Kunstbehoud* VI (1996), no. 3, pp. 8-10

DEVISSCHER 1992 H. Devisscher, 'Die Entstehung der Waldlandschaft in den Niederlanden', in: *Von Bruegel bis Rubens. Das goldene Jahrhundert der flämischen Malerei*, Cologne (Wallraf-Richartz-Museum), 1992, pp. 191-202

DÜLBERG 1990 A. Dülberg, *Privatporträts. Geschichte und Ikonologie einer Gattung im 15. und 16. Jahrhundert*, Berlin 1990

DUNKERTON ET AL. 1991 J. Dunkerton et al., *Giotto to Dürer. Early Renaissance Painting in the National Gallery*, London 1991

EHRESMANN 1982 D.L. Ehresmann, 'Some observations on the role of liturgy in the early winged altarpiece', *Art Bulletin* LXIV (1982), pp. 359-69

FALKENBURG 1988 R.L. Falkenburg, *Joachim Patinir. Landscape as an image of the Pilgrimage of Life*, Amsterdam/Philadelphia 1988

FRIEDLÄNDER 1915 M.J. Friedländer, 'Die Antwerpener Manieristen von 1520', *Jahrbuch der königlich preussischen Kunstsammlungen* XXXVI (1915), pp. 65-91

FRIEDLÄNDER 1917 M.J. Friedländer, 'Der Meister von Frankfurt', *Jahrbuch der königlich preussischen Kunstsammlungen* XXXVIII (1917), pp. 135-50

FRIEDLÄNDER 1924-25 M.J. Friedländer, 'Der Meister der Barbara-Legende', *Jahrbuch für Kunstwissenschaft* I (1924-25), pp. 21-25

FRIEDLÄNDER 1924-37 M.J. Friedländer, *Die altniederländische Malerei*, I-XIV, Berlin/Leiden 1924-37

FRIEDLÄNDER 1939 M.J. Friedländer, 'Der Meister von Sainte Gudule. Nachträgliches', *Annuaire des Musées Royaux des Beaux-Arts de Belgique* II (1939), p. 23-31

FRIEDLÄNDER 1967-76 M.J. Friedländer, *Early Netherlandish Painting*, I-XIV, Leiden/Brussels 1967-76

FRIEDLÄNDER/ROOSENBERG 1978 M.J. Friedländer, J. Roosenberg, *The paintings of Lucas Cranach*, London 1978

FRIEDMANN 1946 H. Friedmann, *The symbolic Goldfinch*, Washington 1946

FRIEDMANN 1980 H. Friedmann, *A Bestiary for Saint Jerome. Animal Symbolism in European Religious Art*, Washington 1980

VAN GELDER-SCHRIJVER N.F. van Gelder-Schrijver, 'De Meester van Alkmaar', *Oud Holland* XLVII (1930), pp. 97-121

GENAILLE 1986 R. Genaille, 'Le paysage flamand et wallon au XVIème siècle avant Patenier', *Jaarboek Koninklijk Museum voor Schone Kunsten Antwerpen*, 1986, pp. 59-82

GIBSON 1987 W.S. Gibson, 'Jan Gossaert: the Lisbon triptych reconsidered', *Simiolus* XVII (1987), pp. 79-89

GIBSON 1989 W.S. Gibson, *'Mirror of the Earth' The World Landscape in Sixteenth-Century Flemish Painting*, Princeton 1989

GLAVIMANS 1946 A. Glavimans, 'Notities bij de primitieven in het Mauritshuis. Nederlandsche kunst van de 15e en 16e eeuw', *Phoenix* I (1946), no. 1, pp. 46-57

GODDARD 1983 S.H. Goddard, *The Master of Frankfurt and his Shop*, I-II (diss.), University of Iowa 1983

GODDARD 1984 S.H. Goddard, *The Master of Frankfurt and his Shop* (Verhandelingen van de Koninklijke Academie voor Wetenschappen, Letteren en Schone Kunsten van België, Klasse der Schone Kunsten, XLVI, no. 38), Brussels 1984

GODDARD 1985 S.H. Goddard, 'Brocade Patterns in the Shop of the Master of Frankfurt: An Accessory to Stylistic Analysis', *Art Bulletin* LXVII (1985), pp. 401-17

GOOSEN 1990 L. Goosen, *Van Abraham tot Zacharias. Thema's uit het Oude Testament in religie, beeldende kunst, literatuur, muziek en theater*, Nijmegen 1990

GOOSEN 1992 L. Goosen, *Van Andreas tot Zacheüs. Thema's uit het Nieuwe Testament en de apocriefe literatuur in religie en kunsten*, The Hague 1992

GUISLAIN-WITTERMAN 1978-79 R. Guislain-Witterman, 'L'Œuvre-clef du Maître de la Légende de Sainte Barbe. Genèse technologique', *Bulletin de l'Institut Royal du Patrimoine Artistique* XVII (1978-79), pp. 89-105

GULDAN 1966 E. Guldan, *Eva und Maria. Eine Antithese als Bildmotiv*, Graz/Cologne 1966

HAASSE 1989 H. Haasse, 'Gerard David, *Bosgezicht*', in: H.R. Hoetink (ed.), *Gezicht op het Mauritshuis. Poëtische visies op een uitzonderlijk museum*, The Hague 1989, pp. 63-67

HÄNSCHKE 1988 U. Hänschke, *Die Flämische Waldlandschaft. Anfänge und Entwicklungen im 16. und 17. Jahrhundert*, Worms 1988

THE HAGUE 1945 *Nederlandsche kunst van de XVde en XVIde eeuw*, The Hague (Mauritshuis), 1945

HALL 1979 J. Hall, *Dictionary of Subjects and Symbols in Art*, revised edition, New York/San Francisco/London 1979

HAND/WOLFF 1986 J.O. Hand, M. Wolff, *The collection of the National Gallery of Art. Systematic Catalogue. Early Netherlandish Painting*, Washington 1986

HARBISON 1990 C. Harbison, 'The northern altarpiece as a cultural document', in: Humfrey/Kemp 1990, pp. 49-75

HARBISON 1995 C. Harbison, *The Mirror of the Artist. Northern Renaissance Art in its Historical Context*, New York 1995

HÄRTING 1995 U. Härting, 'Bilder der Bibel. Gerard Davids "Waldlandschaften mit Ochsen und Esel" (um 1509) und Pieter Bruegels "Landschaft mit wilden Tieren"', *Niederdeutsche Beiträge zur Kunstgeschichte* XXXIV (1995), pp. 81-105

HAVERKAMP BEGEMANN/CHONG 1985 E. Haverkamp Begemann, A. Chong, 'Dutch landscape and its associations', in: Hoetink 1985, pp. 56-67

HEIL 1929 W. Heil, 'The Jules Bache Collection', *Art News* XXVII (1929), pp. 3-33

HELLER 1976 E. Heller, *Das altniederländisches Stifterbild*, Munich 1976

HENKELS 1993 H. Henkels, 'De collectie Hoogendijk (1866-1911)', *Bulletin van het Rijksmuseum* XLI (1993), pp. 155-287

HOETINK 1985 H.R. Hoetink (ed.), *The Royal Picture Gallery Mauritshuis*, Amsterdam/New York/The Hague 1985

HOETINK/DUPARC 1977 *Mauritshuis. The Royal Cabinet of Paintings. Illustrated General Catalogue*, The Hague 1977

HOFF/DAVIES 1971 U. Hoff, M. Davies, *Les Primitifs Flamands, The National Gallery of Victoria, Melbourne* XII, Brussels 1971

HOLLSTEIN (GERMAN) *F.W.H. Hollstein's German Etchings, Engravings and Woodcuts ca. 1400-1700*, I-XLIII (continued), Amsterdam/Roosendaal/Rotterdam 1954-96

HOLLSTEIN 1996 G. Luijten (ed.), *The new Hollstein Dutch and Flemish Etchings, Engravings and Woodcuts 1450-1700 Lucas van Leyden*, Rotterdam 1996

HOOGEWERFF 1936-47 G.J. Hoogewerff, *De Noord-Nederlandsche schilderkunst*, I-V, The Hague 1936-47

HULIN DE LOO 1923 G. Hulin de Loo, 'Diptychs by Rogier van der Weyden', *Burlington Magazine* XLIII (1923), pp. 53-58

HUMFREY/KEMP 1990 P. Humfrey, M. Kemp (ed.), *The Altarpiece in the Renaissance*, Cambridge 1990

JACOBS 1986 L. Jacobs, *Aspects of Netherlandish Carved Altarpieces*, New York 1986

JACOBS 1994 L. Jacobs, 'The Commissioning of Early Netherlandish Carved Altarpieces', *A Tribute to Robert A. Koch: Studies in the Northern Renaissance*, Princeton 1994, pp. 83-114

JANSON 1952 H.W. Janson, *Apes and Ape Lore in the Middle Ages and the Renaissance*, London 1952

DE JONG 1985 M.J.G. de Jong, *Vrede en vrolicheyt: kerstfeest in de Middeleeuwen*, Baarn 1985

KIRSCHBAUM/BRAUNFELS 1968-76 E. Kirschbaum, F. Braunfels, *Lexikon der Christlichen Ikonografie*, I-VIII, Rome/Freiburg/Basel/Vienna 1968-76

KLEIN 1994 P. Klein, 'Dendrochronological analysis of panels of Hans Memling', in: Bruges 1994, pp. 101-03

KNIPPING 1942 B. Knipping, *Hoe kerstlegenden kwamen en gingen. Over de ontwikkeling van de kerstvoorstelling*, Hilversum 1942

KOCH 1968 R. Koch, *Joachim Patinir*, Princeton 1968

KOFUKU 1990 A. Kofuku, 'Landschape with Virgin and Child or Rest on the Flight into Egypt – Patinir and Early Flemish Painting', in: *Bruegel and Netherlandish Landscape Painting from the National Gallery Prague*, Tokyo (The National Museum of Western Art), Kyoto (The National Museum of Modern Art), 1990, pp. 37-47

VAN DER LAAN 1990 P.W.A.T. van der Laan, *Sedulius Carmen Paschale Boek 4. Inleiding, vertaling, commentaar* (diss.), Leiden 1990

LAEMERS 1995 S.A.M. Laemers, *De triptiek als liturgisch gebruiksvoorwerp. Kwantitatief onderzoek naar de themakeuze en de vertelstructuur van de Zuidnederlandse triptiek, 1390-1530* (typescript), Nijmegen 1995

LANE 1975 B.G. Lane, 'Ecce Panis Angelorum. The Manger as Altar in Hugo's Berlin *Nativity*', *Art Bulletin* LVII (1975), pp. 477-86

LANE 1984 B.G. Lane, *The Altar and the Altarpiece. Sacramental Themes in Early Netherlandish Painting*, New York 1984

LARSEN 1960 E. Larsen, *Les Primitifs Flamands au Musée Métropolitain de New York*, Utrecht/Antwerp 1960

LEFÈVRE/PRAEM 1936 P. Lefèvre, O. Praem, 'Mélanges. A propos de "L'Instruction Pastorale" du Louvre', *Revue Belge d'Architecture et d'Histoire de l'Art* VI (1936), p. 359

LENINGRAD/MOSCOW 1975 *Hundred Paintings from the Metropolitan Museum*, Leningrad (Hermitage), Moscow (Pushkin Museum), 1975

LEVI D'ANCONA 1977 M. Levi d'Ancona, *The Garden of the Renaissance. Botanical Symbolism in Italian Painting*, Florence 1977

LONDON 1949 *Gerard David and his followers*, London (Wildenstein Gallery), 1949

LOUCHHEIM 1945-46 A.B. Louchheim, '5,000 Years of Art. Survey of the Metropolitan's Collections', *Art News Annual* XLIV (1945-46), pp. 7-114

LUIJTEN 1984 G. Luijten, '"De veelheid en de eelheid" een Rijksmuseum Schmidt-Degener', *Nederlands Kunsthistorisch Jaarboek* XXXV (1984), pp. 351-429

MAK 1948 J. Mak, *Middeleeuwse kerstvoorstellingen*, Utrecht/Brussels 1948

VAN MANDER/MIEDEMA 1994-96 H. Miedema, *Karel van Mander The Lives of the Illustrious Netherlandish and German Painters, from the first edition of the* Schilder-boeck *(1603-1604)*, I-III, Doornspijk 1994-96

MARLIER 1957 G. Marlier, *Ambrosius Benson et la peinture à Bruges au temps de Charles-Quint*, Damme 1957

MARROW 1979 J. Marrow, *Passion Iconography in Northern European Art of the Late Middle Ages and Early Renaissance*, Courtrai 1979

MARTIN 1935 W. Martin, *Musée royal de tableaux Mauritshuis à La Haye. Catalogue raisonné des tableaux et sculptures*, The Hague 1935

MAYER 1920 A.L. Mayer, 'Ein unbekanntes Triptychon von Gerard David', *Zeitschrift für Bildende Kunst* LV (1920), p. 97

MAYER 1930 A.L. Mayer, 'Die Sammlung Jules Bache in New-York', *Pantheon* VI (1930), pp. 537-42

MEISS 1936 M. Meiss, 'The Madonna of Humility', *Art Bulletin* XVIII (1936), pp. 435-64

MICHEL 1953 E. Michel, *Musée National du Louvre*, Paris 1953

VAN MIEGROET 1989 H.J. Van Miegroet, *Gerard David*, Antwerp 1989

MOLL 1854 W. Moll, *Johannes Brugman en het godsdienstig leven onzer vaderen in de vijftiende eeuw*, I-II, Amsterdam 1854

MORSE 1979 J.D. Morse, *Old Master Paintings in North America. Over 3000 Masterpieces by 50 Great Artists*, New York 1979

MULLER 1985 E. Muller, 'Heilige maagden. De verering van maagdheiligen in religieuze vrouwengemeenschappen', in: Nijmegen 1985, pp. 83-100

MUNDY 1980 E.J. Mundy III, *Gerard David Studies* (diss.), Princeton 1980

NEILSEN BLUM 1969 S. Neilsen Blum, *Early Netherlandish Triptychs: A Study in Patronage*, Berkeley/Los Angeles 1969

NIEBURG 1946 P. Nieburg, 'Twee boschgezichten van Gerard David', *Constghesellen* I (1946), pp. 16-17

NIJMEGEN 1985 *Tussen heks en heilige. Het vrouwbeeld op de drempel van de moderne tijd, 15de/16de eeuw*, Nijmegen (Commanderie van Sint-Jan), 1985

NIKULIN 1987 N. Nikulin, *Netherlandish Paintings in Soviet Museums*, Leningrad/Oxford 1987

NIKULIN 1989 N. Nikulin, *The Hermitage. Catalogue of Western European Painting. Netherlandish Painting Fifteenth and Sixteenth Centuries*, Florence 1989

VAN OS 1990 H.W. van Os, 'Some thoughts on writing a history of Sienese altarpieces', in: Humfrey/Kemp 1990, pp. 21-33

VON DER OSTEN/VEY 1969 G. von der Osten, H. Vey, *Painting and Sculpture in Germany and the Netherlands 1500 to 1600*, Middlesex 1969

D'OTRANGE 1951 M.L. d'Otrange, 'Gerard David at the Metropolitan, New York', *Connoisseur* CXXVIII (1951), no. 524, pp. 206-11

VAN OUDHEUSDEN 1988 J. van Oudheusden, *De Sint Jan van 's-Hertogenbosch*, Zwolle 1988

PANOFSKY 1945 E. Panofsky, *Albrecht Dürer*, I-II, London 1945

PANOFSKY 1953 E. Panofsky, *Early Netherlandish Painting. Its Origins and Character*, I-II, Cambridge (Mass.) 1953

PARIS 1935 *De Van Eyck à Bruegel*, Paris (Musée de l'Orangerie), 1935

PÉRIER-D'IETEREN 1989-91 C. Périer-d'Ieteren, 'Le "Retable du Martyre des saints Crépin et Crépinien" et le Maître de la Légende de sainte Barbe', *Bulletin Musées Royaux des Beaux-Arts de Belgique, Bruxelles* 1989-91, pp. 157-74

PÉRIER-D'IETEREN 1994 C. Périer-d'Ieteren, 'Apports à l'étude du triptyche de Melbourne: II. La *Multiplication des pains*, La *Résurrection de Lazare*, La *Fuite en Égypte* et *Saint Pierre*', *Annales d'Histoire de l'Art et d'Archéologie* XVI (1994), pp. 47-78

POCHAT 1973 G. Pochat, *Figur und landschaft*, Berlin/New York 1973

POTTASCH 1994 C. Pottasch, 'Jan Provoost (ca 1465-1529) Triptych with Madonna and Child (central panel) John the Evangelist and Mary Magdalene (wings)', *Mauritshuis in Focus* VII (1994), no. 1, pp. 14-17

VAN PUYVELDE 1947 L. Van Puyvelde, *Les Primitifs Flamands*, Paris (Musée de l'Orangerie), 1947

VAN PUYVELDE 1968 L. Van Puyvelde, *La peinture flamande des Van Eyck à Metsys*, Brussels 1968

RAGGHIANTI 1990 L.C. Ragghianti, *Dipinti Fiamminghi in Italia 1420-1570. Catalogo*, Bologna/Rome/Milan 1990

RAGUSA/GREEN 1961 I. Ragusa, R.B. Green (eds), *Meditations on the Life of Christ, an illustrated manuscript of the fourteenth century*, Princeton 1961

RÉAU 1955-59 L. Réau, *Iconographie de l'art chrétien*, I-VI, Paris 1955-59

REYNAUD/FOUCART 1970 N. Reynaud, J. Foucart, 'Primitifs flamands anonymes', *Revue de l'Art* VIII (1970), pp. 67-72

RICE 1985 E.F. Rice, *Saint Jerome in the Renaissance*, Baltimore 1985

RIDDERBOS 1991 B. Ridderbos, *De melancholie van de kunstenaar. Hugo van der Goes en de Oudnederlandse schilderkunst*, The Hague 1991

RIDDERBOS 1995 B. Ridderbos, 'Objecten en vragen', in: R. Ridderbos, H. van Veen (eds), *'Om iets te weten van de oude meesters'. De Vlaamse Primitieven – herontdekking, waardering en onderzoek*, Nijmegen 1995, pp. 15-133

RIETSTAP 1884-87 J.B. Rietstap, *Armorial Général*, I-II, Gouda 1884-87

RIETSTAP/ROLLAND 1903-26 J.B. Rietstap, V. Rolland, *Planches de l'Armorial Général de J.B. Rietstap*, I-VI, Paris/The Hague 1903-26

ROBERTS 1987 A.M. Roberts, 'The Lucy Master and Hugo van der Goes', *Jaarboek Koninklijk Museum voor Schone Kunsten Antwerpen* 1987, pp. 9-24

ROHLMANN 1995 M. Rohlmann, 'Memlings's "Pagagnotti triptych"', *Burlington Magazine* CXXXVII (1995), no. 1108, pp. 438-45

ROTH-BOJADZHIEV 1985 G. Roth-Bojadzhiev, *Studien zur Bedeutung der Vögel in der mittelalterlichen Tafelmalerei*, Cologne/Vienna 1985

ROTTERDAM 1965 *Jan Gossaert*, Rotterdam (Museum Boymans-van Beuningen), 1965

SANDER 1993 J. Sander, *Niederländische Gemälde im Städel 1400-1500*, Mainz am Rhein 1993

SCHÖNE 1938 W. Schöne, *Dieric Bouts und seine Schule*, Berlin/Leipzig 1938

SCHWARTZ 1975 S. Schwartz, *The Iconography of the Rest on the Flight to Egypt* (diss.), New York 1975

SCILLIA 1975 D.G. Scillia, *Gerard David and Manuscript Illumination in the Low Countries, 1480-1509* (diss.), Cleveland 1975

SLUIJTER-SEIJFFERT ET AL. 1993 N.C. Sluijter-Seijffert et al., *Mauritshuis. Illustrated General Catalogue*, Amsterdam/The Hague 1993

SMITS 1933 K. Smits, *Iconografie van de Nederlandsche Primitieven*, Amsterdam/Brussels/Antwerp/Louvain 1933

SNYDER 1985 J. Snyder, *Northern Renaissance Art. Painting, Sculpture, The Graphic Arts from 1350 to 1575*, New York 1985

SPRONK 1993 R. Spronk, *Jan Provoost Art Historical and Technical Examinations* (typescript), I-II, Groningen 1993

STADLER 1936 F. Stadler, *Hans von Kulmbach*, Vienna 1936

STECHOW 1966 W. Stechow, *Dutch Landscape Painting of the Seventeenth Century*, London 1966

STEINMETZ 1993 A.S. Steinmetz, *Das Altarretabel in der altniederländischen Malerei* (diss.), Cologne 1993

TEASDALE SMITH 1959 M. Teasdale Smith, 'The use of grisaille as a Lenten observation', *Marsyas* VIII (1959), pp. 43-54

DE TERVARENT 1936 G. de Tervarent, 'Sur quatre primitifs exposés à Bruxelles', *Gazette des Beaux-Arts* LXXVIII (1936), pp. 52-56

VAN THIEL ET AL. 1976 P.J.J. van Thiel et al., *All the paintings of the Rijksmuseum in Amsterdam. A completely illustrated catalogue*, Amsterdam 1976

THIERRY DE BYE DÓLLEMAN 1965 M. Thierry de Bye Dólleman, 'Het geslacht Van Soutelande', *Jaarboek van het Centraal Bureau voor Genealogie* 1965, pp. 1-24

TIMMERS 1974 J.J.M. Timmers, *Christelijke symboliek en iconografie*, Bussum 1974

TÓTH-UBBENS 1968 M.M. Tóth-Ubbens, *Schilderijen en beeldhouwwerken 15e en 16e eeuw. Catalogus 1. Koninklijk Kabinet van Schilderijen Mauritshuis*, The Hague 1968

UDEN 1992 T. Brandenbarg et al., *Heilige Anna, grote moeder. De cultus van de Heilige Moeder Anna en haar familie in de Nederlanden en aangrenzende streken*, Uden (Museum voor Religieuze kunst), 1992

UTRECHT 1988 M. Caron (ed.), *Helse en hemelse vrouwen. Schrikbeelden en voorbeelden van de vrouw in de christelijke cultuur*, Utrecht (Rijksmuseum Het Catharijneconvent), 1988

VIGNAU WILBERG-SCHUURMAN T. Vignau Wilberg-Schuurman, *Hoofse minne en burgerlijke liefde in de prentkunst rond 1500*, Leiden 1983

VLIEGHE 1985 H. Vlieghe, 'Flemish painting from the 15th to the 17th century', in: Hoetink 1985, pp. 102-16

VLOBERG 1946 M. Vloberg, *L'Eucharistie dans l'art*, Grenoble/Paris 1946

VOGELAAR 1987 C. Vogelaar, *Netherlandish Fifteenth and Sixteenth Century Paintings in the National Gallery of Ireland*, Dublin 1987

DE VOS 1994 Dirk De Vos, *Hans Memling. Het volledige œuvre*, Antwerp 1994

WEHLE 1943 H.B. Wehle, 'The Bache Collection on Loan', *The Metropolitan Museum of Art Bulletin* I (1943), no. 10, pp. 285-90

WEHLE/SALINGER 1947 H.B. Wehle, M. Salinger, *A Catalogue of Early Flemish, Dutch and German Paintings. The Metropolitan Museum of Art*, New York 1947

WEISZÄCKER 1897 H. Weiszäcker, 'Der Meister von Frankfurt', *Zeitschrift für christliche Kunst* X (1897), pp. 1-16

WERTHEIM AYMÈS 1957 C.A. Wertheim Aymès, *Hieronymus Bosch. Eine Einführung in seine geheime Symbolik*, Amsterdam 1957

WERTHEIM AYMÈS 1961 C.A. Wertheim Aymès, *Die Bildersprache des Hieronymus Bosch*, The Hague 1961

WHINNEY 1968 M. Whinney, *Early Flemish painting*, London 1968

WILSON 1995 J.C. Wilson, 'Adriaen Isenbrant and the Problem of his Œuvre', *Oud Holland* CIX (1995), pp. 1-17

WINKLER 1924 F. Winkler, *Die altniederländische Malerei*, Berlin 1924

WINKLER 1959 F. Winkler, *Hans von Kulmbach. Leben und Werk eines fränkischen Künstlers der Dürerzeit*, Kulmbach 1959

WINKLER 1964 F. Winkler, *Das Werk des Hugo van der Goes*, Berlin 1964

WOOD 1993 C.S. Wood, *Albrecht Altdorfer and the Origins of Landscape*, London 1993

YOUNG 1921 K. Young, '"Ordo Phrophetarum"', *Transactions of the Wisconsin Academy of Sciences, Arts and Letters* XXX (1921), pp. 1-82

YOUNG 1933 K. Young, *The Drama of the Medieval Church*, I-II, Oxford 1933

ZIEGLER 1952 J. Ziegler, 'Ochs und Esel an der Krippe. Biblisch-patristische Erwägungen zu Is 1,3 und Hab. 3,2 (LXX)', *Münchener Theologische Zeitschrift* III (1952), pp. 385-402

Colophon

Translation
Wendie Shaffer, Donald Gardner and Michèle Hendricks

Editing
Ariane van Suchtelen, with the assistance of Quentin Buvelot

Photography
A.C.L.-Brussels (p. 16, fig. 3, p. 44, fig. 1), Jörg P. Anders, Berlin (p. 17, fig. 4), A. Bötefür, Landesamt für Denkmalpflege Mecklenburg-Vorpommern, Schwerin (p. 8, fig. 4), Ed Brandon, The Hague (cat. 1 (Forest Scene), 2, 3, 4a, 5, 6, 7, 10), Courtauld Institute of Art, London (p. 62, figs 3, 4), IRPA-KIK, Brussels (p. 67, fig. 1), Museumsfoto B.P. Keiser (p. 78, fig. 1), H. Maertens, Bruges (cat. 8)

Design
Cees de Jong and Corine Teuben, V+K Design, Bussum

Printing
bv Kunstdrukkerij Mercurius-Wormerveer